Penguin Monarchs

THE HOUSES OF WESSEX AND DENMARK

Athelstan	Tom Holland
Aethelred the Unready	Richard Abels
Cnut	Ryan Lavelle

THE HOUSES OF NORMANDY, BLOIS AND ANJOU

William I	Marc Morris
William II	John Gillingham
Henry I	Edmund King
Stephen	Carl Watkins
Henry II	Richard Barber
Richard I	Thomas Asbridge
John	Nicholas Vincent

THE HOUSE OF PLANTAGENET

Henry III	Stephen Church
Edward I	Andy King
Edward II	Christopher Given-Wilson
Edward III	Jonathan Sumption
Richard II	Laura Ashe

THE HOUSES OF LANCASTER AND YORK

Henry IV	Catherine Nall
Henry V	Anne Curry
Henry VI	James Ross
Edward IV	A. J. Pollard
Edward V	Thomas Penn
Richard III	Rosemary Horrox

THE HOUSE OF TUDOR

Henry VII	Sean Cunningham
Henry VIII	John Guy
Edward VI	Stephen Alford
Mary I	John Edwards
Elizabeth I	Helen Castor

THE HOUSE OF STUART

James I	Thomas Cogswell
Charles I	Mark Kishlansky
[Cromwell	David Horspool]
Charles II	Clare Jackson
James II	David Womersley
William III & Mary II	Jonathan Keates
Anne	Richard Hewlings

THE HOUSE OF HANOVER

George I	Tim Blanning
George II	Norman Davies
George III	Amanda Foreman
George IV	Stella Tillyard
William IV	Roger Knight
Victoria	Jane Ridley

THE HOUSES OF SAXE-COBURG & GOTHA AND WINDSOR

Edward VII	Richard Davenport-Hines
George V	David Cannadine
Edward VIII	Piers Brendon
George VI	Philip Ziegler
Elizabeth II	Douglas Hurd

THOMAS ASBRIDGE

Richard I

The Crusader King

ALLEN LANE
an imprint of
PENGUIN BOOKS

ALLEN LANE

UK | USA | Canada | Ireland | Australia
India | New Zealand | South Africa

Penguin Books is part of the Penguin Random House group of companies
whose addresses can be found at global.penguinrandomhouse.com

First published 2018
001

Set in 9.5/13.5 pt Sabon LT Std
Typeset by Jouve (UK), Milton Keynes
Printed in Great Britain by Clays Ltd, St Ives plc

ISBN: 978–0–141–97685–3

www.greenpenguin.co.uk

Contents

For my mother
Gerd Asbridge

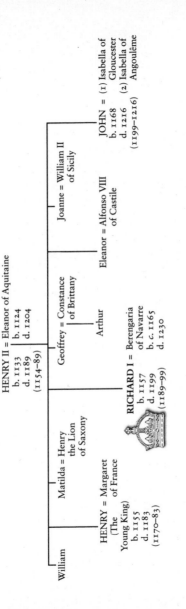

William

HENRY = Margaret
(The   of France
Young King)
b. 1155
d. 1183
(1170–83)

Matilda = Henry
          the Lion
          of Saxony

HENRY II = Eleanor of Aquitaine
b. 1133   b. 1124
d. 1189   d. 1204
(1154–89)

Geoffrey = Constance
           of Brittany

Arthur

RICHARD I = Berengaria
b. 1157   of Navarre
d. 1199   b. c. 1165
(1189–99)   d. 1230

Eleanor = Alfonso VIII
          of Castile

Joanne = William II
         of Sicily

JOHN = (1) Isabella of
b. 1168   Gloucester
d. 1216 (2) Isabella of
(1199–1216) Angoulême

Richard I

I

In Search of the Lionheart

Just before dawn on 5 August 1192, Richard I of England lay sleeping in his resplendent royal tent on the coast of the Holy Land, two thousand miles from home. Unbeknownst to the king, a large party of Muslim warriors were at that moment stealing their way through the half-light, planning to launch a surprise attack and take him prisoner. They might well have succeeded had it not been for a lone Christian sentry, who spotted the first rays of sunlight glinting from their helmets as they approached and immediately raised the alarm. With the camp thrown into frenzied confusion, Richard leapt from his bed, hurriedly pulled on a mail shirt and rushed out to give battle.

The odds that day were not in the king's favour. Only ten of his knights actually had horses, leaving the remaining seventy or so to fight on foot alongside a small force of crossbowmen and assorted infantry – all against an enemy numbering in the thousands, most of whom were mounted. A different man might have contemplated flight, but Richard chose to make a desperate and daring stand, fighting from first light until dusk. Contemporary chroniclers marvelled at his bravery and prowess: 'never was such a battle seen' remarked one, while another likened the king to a 'ferocious lion' felling all in his path. The king's expertise as a military commander was severely tested, but he managed to impose order, throwing up a defensive shield and spear wall, behind which his crossbowmen could operate to good effect, strafing the enemy.

At one point, as the melee reached fever pitch, Richard was said to have 'charged into the accursed people, so that he was swallowed up by them and none of his men could see him'. Brandishing his 'sword with rapid strokes', the king began 'cutting [the enemy] in two as he encountered them', mowing them down 'as if he were harvesting them with a sickle' – carrying himself all the while 'with indescribable vigour and superhuman courage'. At last he emerged from the fray, 'his body completely covered with arrows, which stuck out [from his armour] like the spines of a hedgehog', having shattered the enemy's morale. By day's end, the Muslim army had been driven from the field, leaving behind more than 700 troops and 1,500 horses 'lying scattered everywhere through the fields'.[1]

In many respects, this remarkable military encounter – played out near the port of Jaffa during the closing stages of a hard-fought war for control of the Holy Land – reveals Richard I in all his glory. Here is the English sovereign as a crusader, battling on the fringes of the known world; the warrior-king, possessed of unrivalled martial genius, able to achieve victory no matter the enemy faced. Here too is Richard the knight, fearless and indomitable: skilful (and perhaps foolhardy) enough to fight as a champion in his own right – endowed with the heart of a lion. And here, perhaps most importantly of all, is Richard caught somewhere between fact and fiction – a figure living half in the realm of history, yet also conjured from the mists of myth and legend.

Looking back from the distance of more than eight centuries, we might imagine the stirring tale of King Richard's deeds outside Jaffa to be pure invention – a grandiose story, manufactured by fawning court historians. But independent Arabic sources confirm the broad details of the confrontation, with one Muslim contemporary noting that the Christians fought like snarling 'dogs of war ... willing to battle to the death', and another admitting that Richard rode out alone, ahead of his troops, to seek battle.[2] The earliest Western European accounts of the fighting were written by chroniclers who had travelled to the Near East with the crusading army. These were men with a detailed knowledge of events, but also a desire to promote the achievements of their king and a willingness to embroider their narratives. Their testimony, in common with much of the contemporary evidence for Richard I's life, presents a version of events grounded in reality, yet sometimes interwoven with heightened elements of hyperbole and even fantasy. One challenge, therefore, of charting the course of Richard's career is teasing apart the myth and the man.

This task is rendered no easier by the fact that King Richard I did indeed enjoy an extraordinary, if short, reign. His was a flame that burned briefly, but brightly. It would seem that many of his contemporaries were moved to describe him as a hero for the ages – a rival to Achilles or a match for Alexander the Great – because, in some respects at least, he had actually earned this praise. No other king of England ever led so grand a military campaign, to such far-flung shores. Richard's leadership of the expedition to reconquer Palestine and reclaim the city of Jerusalem from Islam propelled him on to the world stage. This war – now known to history as the Third Crusade – saw him pitted against the mighty Muslim sultan Saladin in a titanic contest for control of the Holy Land, earning Richard fame and renown to eclipse that achieved by any of his predecessors.

The course and consequences of the crusade dominated Richard's ten-year reign. From the moment he ascended the throne in 1189, his mind was bent upon the prosecution of this military campaign and all the resources of his realm were directed to this end. Yet, for all of the king's energy and determination, his masterful generalship and many feats of arms, the conflict ended in stalemate, with Jerusalem unconquered, in 1192. Richard's devotion to the holy war raises a number of essential questions. Why did a king of England devote so much to such a distant cause? Was the expedition pure folly, a selfish quest for glory or a religious obligation? And how can it be that Richard is remembered as one of Western Europe's greatest crusade leaders when he failed to achieve outright victory in the East?

Had King Richard been able to make an immediate return to England in late 1192, the shape of his career might have been radically altered. As it was, he was taken prisoner by a political rival while travelling through Austria and remained in captivity until 1194. Back at home,

Richard's enemies – his duplicitous younger brother John and the King of France, Philip II Augustus – capitalized upon his incarceration, conspiring to overthrow his rule and seize his territory. Once released, Richard was forced to fight for the next four years to reclaim his realm. Much of this struggle was played out on the continent, in the territorial equivalent of modern-day France. When taken together with his absence on crusade and in prison, this meant that Richard spent only a tiny proportion of his reign in England – less perhaps than any other English monarch. Should Richard therefore be branded a neglectful king – a sovereign who cared little for his kingdom and ransacked its resources to fund his foreign wars?

Richard I's reign was brought to an abrupt and premature end in 1199. In the midst of besieging an insignificant castle in south-western France, the king was fatally wounded by a crossbow bolt. His seemingly insatiable appetite for front-line battle cost him his life, but the nature of his demise reflected a deeper truth about his career. Richard conceived of himself not just as a king, but also as a knight: as a warrior-general who could not only lead men in battle, but also wield sword, lance and crossbow with his own hands to deadly effect. In this, he was the product (and perhaps the epitome) of his age, for Richard was born into a culture newly obsessed with the notion of chivalry – one in which prowess was esteemed and honour craved; where a man's value might be gauged by his reputation and measured by the admiration of his peers. Richard seems to have been driven by a raw passion for action, but he was also moved, like so many of his contemporaries, by a gnawing hunger for chivalric recognition and a deeply felt need to avoid shame and dishonour. Perhaps all monarchs aspire to make their mark, but Richard sought to draw the gaze of the world not just as a king, but as a knight. He actively cultivated the sense of awe and mystique that came to surround his career, revelling in the nickname that was already in common usage during his lifetime: *Coeur de Lion*, the Lionheart.

Richard's quest for fame and glory as a warrior proved remarkably successful. After his death, he was lauded as a paragon of chivalric virtue throughout the Middle Ages, and in the modern era even those scholars who might censure other facets of his character have conceded that he was 'a peerlessly efficient killing machine'.[3] But considerable debate remains about the precise quality of the Lionheart's military leadership, not least because – regardless of his fascination with the precepts of chivalry – Richard perpetrated a number of acts of extreme violence: most infamously, the cold-blooded execution of close to 3,000 Muslim prisoners in a single day during the Third Crusade. What manner of commander was he, then: a reckless brute, governed by a raging temper; or a deft mastermind and consummate professional? Perhaps Richard's much-celebrated status as one of the finest generals of the medieval era must itself be contested, given that the contemporary evidence for so many of his achievements was infused with elements of exaggeration and even myth.

The search for the real Lionheart begins in 1157, with his birth into the mightiest and most dysfunctional family in

Europe. To begin with, Richard was not the presumptive heir to the crown, but rather the fourth-born child and second surviving son of King Henry II of England and Queen Eleanor of Aquitaine. The union between the Lionheart's illustrious parents endowed the nascent Angevin dynasty (so called because of Henry II's hereditary status as Count of Anjou) with extraordinary power. Together they could lay claim to lands that included all of England and a vast swathe of territory across the Channel, sweeping in an arc from the duchy of Normandy in the north, south through the regions of Maine and Touraine, to the duchy of Aquitaine and the fringes of the Iberian Peninsula. This immediately placed them at odds with the rather enfeebled titular King of France, the Capetian monarch Louis VII, whose own lands were dwarfed by the upstart Angevins (even though he was nominally their overlord on the continent) – and who just happened to be Eleanor's recently estranged former husband. The intense rivalry between these two houses – the Angevins and the Capetians – would dominate much of Richard's career, particularly once Louis was succeeded by his considerably more able and ambitious son, Philip II, in 1180.

Richard was not raised to become King of England, nor was he expected to inherit the vast Angevin realm. Indeed, for the first twenty-five years of his life, he was eclipsed by his elder brother, the glamorous Henry the Young King (crowned as co-ruler of England alongside his father in 1170). Richard's own formative years were spent not in England, but in Anjou and Aquitaine. His close association with this latter region was established in 1169 – probably through the influence of his mother – and three years later, once Richard reached the age of fifteen (the medieval equivalent of adulthood), he was formally installed as Duke of Aquitaine.

It was here, then, in south-western France, that Richard was shaped into the ruler he would become. Twelfth-century Aquitaine was a wealthy and cultured region – the home of some of Europe's foremost court singers and poets – and, in the course of his youth, Richard gained a fine appreciation for music and verse, even composing songs of his own. He was also literate, having been tutored in medieval Latin, apparently to a high standard. The fact that Richard was bred as a man of arts and learning might immediately give lie to any suggestion that he was simply a feral brute, but he also received a firm education in the realities of war and power politics through these early years. Proud and independent-minded, the people of Aquitaine were notoriously difficult to govern and far from content to bear the yoke of Angevin rule. Through the 1170s and 1180s, Richard had to quell a series of incipient local rebellions, often through force of arms. This brought him invaluable experience of military command from a very young age and enabled him to garner expertise in two staples of medieval warfare: horse-borne raiding and siege-craft.

Richard also had to contend with the viperous infighting that beset his family. In all, Henry II and Eleanor produced seven children who survived into adulthood, the last of whom – John – was born in 1167. With such a bumper crop of potential heirs and heiresses at his fingertips, Henry looked set to establish the Angevins as an enduring and immensely influential dynasty. His plan was to hold his eldest son and namesake, Young Henry, in the wings as primary successor. Other sons, like Richard, were deployed to govern portions of the burgeoning Angevin empire in his name, while Henry's three daughters were used to secure a complex web of international alliances through marriage. The problem with this handsome scheme was that Henry II was an inveterate hoarder of power, never content to release the reins of government. It was said that, as a young boy, he had been conditioned by his formidable mother, Empress Matilda, to instil loyalty in his servants and subjects not through kindness or generosity, but rather the harsh denial of favour – acting as if he were seeking to tame an 'unruly hawk' by repeatedly offering the bird a reward of meat, only to snatch it away at the last second. With this in mind, Henry – or the Old King, as he came to be known – sought to control the members of his family by keeping them hungry for praise and advancement, while simultaneously sowing seeds of doubt, mutual suspicion and distrust among their number.[4]

Henry the Young King was the first to bridle at this treatment. Sick of being a monarch in name alone, he rebelled against the authority of his father in 1173, instigating a full-blown civil war. With the connivance of Queen Eleanor, Young Henry forged an alliance with his family's arch rival, Louis VII, and sought to seize control of Normandy. Though still just a teenager, Richard fought alongside his elder brother for a time, but by the autumn of 1174 the uprising had been quashed. Young Henry and Richard were eventually forgiven for their transgressions, but Queen Eleanor was taken into confinement for the rest of Henry II's reign. Henry the Young King launched a second attempt to seize power in early 1183, this time targeting Richard's own position in Aquitaine. By this stage, however, the Lionheart was in his mid twenties and already something of a veteran campaigner. He blunted the first force of Young Henry's attempted invasion with ruthless efficiency and then, with the support of the Old King, penned his brother's forces into the city of Limoges.

Young Henry soon met with a rather tragic and squalid end. Thwarted in all his ambitions, the king without a kingdom contracted a severe case of dysentery and died on 11 June 1183. His demise transformed Richard's own position and prospects. No longer the second son, or a mere princeling, he became Henry II's primary heir and the potential successor to not only the kingdom of England, but the entire Angevin realm.

By this stage, Richard had apparently grown into his athletic frame. A contemporary chronicler offered this striking – if somewhat overblown – portrait of his physical appearance:

> He was tall, of elegant build; the colour of his hair was between red and gold; his limbs were supple and straight. He had quite long arms, which were particularly convenient for drawing a sword and wielding it most effectively. His long legs matched the arrangement of his whole body.[5]

Though they had briefly fought together as allies in 1183, the radical shift in the Lionheart's status soon reshaped his relationship with the Old King. Like Young Henry before him, Richard quickly learned that he would have to fight for his right to power, as Henry II threatened to reclaim Aquitaine and even dangled the suggestion that he might designate his youngest son, John, as his heir in England.

From 1187 onwards, Richard waged a two-year war of succession against his ageing father. It soon became clear that the Lionheart was not only maturing into an extremely effective military commander; he also was learning how to prevail in the treacherous game of medieval power politics. To outflank Henry II, Richard established his own devious alliance with the Capetians – now led by King Philip Augustus. Through long months of military campaigning, court intrigue and seemingly interminable rounds of double-dealing and inconclusive negotiation, the Lionheart gradually eroded Henry's previously vice-like grip on power. By the summer of 1189, the Old King had been hounded into a corner; exhausted, and beset by illness, he finally confirmed Richard in his position as heir on 4 July. Just two days later, Henry II died at the castle of Chinon in Touraine.

Around 10 July, the Lionheart came to the abbey church at Fontevraud, where the Old King's body had been laid out in preparation for burial. It was said that Richard's face remained impassive as he looked down upon Henry II's corpse – the father he had fought and eventually betrayed, all in the dogged pursuit of power.[6] It was perhaps in this moment that he felt the immense burden of kingship settling upon his shoulders, but in the eyes of his contemporaries Richard had first to undergo the transformative ritual of coronation before he could truly be regarded as a sovereign. With this in mind, he made for England.

By this time, events in the wider world had lent a real sense of urgency to the Lionheart's movements. In 1187 – just as Richard began to openly challenge the Old King's authority – a conflict was raging in the distant Holy Land. That July, the Western Christian (or Latin) crusader kingdom of Jerusalem was invaded by a 40,000-strong Muslim army, led by the fearsome Kurdish warlord Saladin.* The sultan inflicted a terrible defeat upon the Latins at the Battle of Hattin and went on to reconquer the sacred city of Jerusalem itself. In response to this calamity, the pope preached a new crusade and, in common with most of Europe's ruling aristocracy, Richard enlisted. Debate about the preparations for this grand expedition had rumbled on in the background, even as the contest surrounding the Angevin succession intensified, but now that the Lionheart had achieved victory at home, he was keen to embark upon his crusade.

Pausing only briefly to confer with King Philip of France and to receive his investiture as Duke of Normandy in Rouen, Richard arrived in England in mid August. On Sunday 3 September 1189, his coronation was celebrated in Westminster Abbey. A contemporary chronicler made a precise record of the ceremony. This extraordinarily detailed account of the elaborate rituals involved in the

---

* Medieval European Christians are most accurately referred to as 'Latins' because of the language of their scripture and ritual.

making of an English king provides the clearest picture of a coronation since the time of the Norman Conquest, and it reveals a fascinating fusion of ecclesiastical and secular elements.[7]

Richard arrived at the entrance to what was then the abbey church of St Peter at Westminster, having processed in state along a woollen carpet from the door of the royal chamber in the neighbouring palace of Westminster. The party was led by a host of chanting clergymen – made up of a mixture of priors, abbots and bishops – bearing 'holy water, the cross, tapers and censers', with four noblemen in their midst carrying golden candlesticks. They were followed by a succession of barons, each holding parts of the royal regalia: the so-called cap of maintenance; a pair of giant golden spurs; the royal sceptre (topped by a cross) and the royal rod (topped by a dove), both wrought from gold. Richard's younger brother John was next, flanked by two magnates – all of them carrying gold-inlaid swords from the royal treasury. Twelve earls and barons followed, bearing a huge chequered wooden board, upon which were laid the royal arms and robes of state, while 'the great and massive crown, decorated on every side with precious stones' was borne by the eminent baron William de Mandeville.* Richard himself walked behind this regal panoply, the Bishops of Durham and Bath at his sides, a silken

---

* This may have been the same huge crown used by King Henry II, but appears to have been distinct from the crown first worn by King Edward the Confessor and traditionally viewed as being the centrepiece of medieval England's royal regalia.

canopy held above their heads on four lofty spears. In the Lionheart's wake came a vast crowd of earls, barons, knights, clergy and assorted members of the laity.

Once inside the abbey church, Richard was led to the altar and the ritual of coronation began in earnest. As the Lionheart knelt, copies of the holy gospels and an assortment of sacred relics were placed before him, and he then swore an oath to 'honour the Church and rule with justice, forsaking unjust laws'. The most critical moment of the whole ceremony came when Richard was stripped to his undershirt and breeches, his chest bared and his feet shod with gold-embroidered sandals. Archbishop Baldwin of Canterbury – the senior churchman in England – then stepped forward to pour holy oil upon Richard's head, chest and arms, each site representing respectively the qualities of knowledge, valour and glory. This act of anointing, which could only ever be performed once in a monarch's life, was the coronation's central drama – the moment at which Richard was deemed to have been remade as a divinely ordained king: God's chosen representative on Earth.

Once anointed, a consecrated linen cloth and the cap of maintenance were placed on the Lionheart's head; he was clothed in his royal raiment, girded with the sword of rule; the golden spurs were affixed to his feet. Richard then picked up the vast crown from the altar, handed it to Archbishop Baldwin, who placed it on the Lionheart's head (though it was apparently so heavy that it had to be held in place by two earls). Carrying the royal sceptre in his right hand and the rod of rule in his left, Richard was finally led back to his throne by two bishops. Mass was then cel-ebrated, during which the new sovereign made the customary offering of 'a single mark of the purest gold' to the Church. With the coronation completed at last, King Richard I walked in state from the abbey church, ready to embark on his new life as monarch of England. He was just five days short of his thirty-second birthday.

2

The Absent King

One startling fact looms over Richard I's career: though among the most renowned of all England's monarchs, the Lionheart spent barely six months on English soil. With such a small proportion of his decade-long reign seemingly dedicated to the care of the realm, it is perhaps little wonder that some sought to criticize Richard's conduct. From the eighteenth century onwards, historians have often painted him as a negligent king – branding him variously as a 'selfish ruler', a figure who 'used England as a bank on which to draw and overdraw in order to finance his ambitious exploits abroad' and, perhaps most damningly of all, as 'one of the worst rulers England has ever had'.[1]

Over time, this scholarly condemnation began to percolate into contemporary culture, colouring some aspects of popular perception. Richard came to be seen as a figure who absented himself from his kingdom in pursuit of glory. *1066 and All That* – the satirical overview of English history penned in the 1930s – mocked his nickname *Coeur de Lion*, declaring that 'whenever he returned to England he always set out again immediately for the Mediterranean and was therefore known as Richard Gare de Lyon'.[2]

In the abiding caricature that gradually took hold, Richard emerged as a ruler who had cared little for his realm but was content to pillage its resources for his own purposes, leaving England weakened and prone to collapse. Exposed to the predations of Richard's conniving younger brother John and the resurgent Capetian French, it was argued, the kingdom was set on an irrevocable path towards the catastrophes of civil war and foreign invasion witnessed in the early thirteenth century. Moreover, Richard the negligent king could also be presented as a foreigner because, arguably, the Lionheart himself was not in any real sense English. Though born in Oxford on 8 September 1157, Richard spent the majority of his formative years on the continent and, in terms of upbringing, culture, language and identity, might just as well be regarded as French. What is to be made of this vision of Richard I? Must the king who was once celebrated as a titan of English history and an emblem of national identity be discarded and replaced by a self-serving foreigner who cared little for England?

French may have been Richard's first language – indeed, he may not have spoken more than a few words of English – but this was true of all of England's kings and most of its nobles from the Norman Conquest till at least the thirteenth century. Since 1066, the kingdom had been ruled as part of a broader realm, with an important continental component. As the son and eventual heir of King Henry II and Queen Eleanor of Aquitaine – the founders of the Angevin dynasty – Richard inherited an even more impressive array of territories, stretching from the Scottish borders in the north to the foothills of the Pyrenees in the south. England was, in almost every respect, the prize jewel of this grand empire: bringing its rulers coveted royal status; catapulting them beyond the world of ordinary men, even of counts or dukes, to become God's anointed representatives on Earth. In relative terms, England was also a law-abiding and wealthy realm, in which the crown's will was heeded and taxes efficiently collected. It would certainly not be true to say that Richard cared little for England or his royal title. In fact, they were essential components of his rank and eminence – prizes for which he had fought and intrigued with bitter determination towards the end of Henry II's life. Richard also seems to have coveted the sense of majesty associated with his office: he was the first King of England to date royal documents with his regnal, rather than calendar, year; and also the first to employ the majestic plural – the so-called 'royal we'.

None the less, Richard's Angevin inheritance brought with it other important lands, titles and responsibilities across the English Channel. From 1189 onwards, he held dominion over a large portion of the territory that constitutes modern-day France, including regions such as Normandy, Anjou, Maine and Aquitaine, controlling far more territory than the French king himself. This fundamental reality meant that the Lionheart reigned throughout his period of office, not simply as a king of England, but rather as ruler of a far larger and more complex realm – one that has sometimes been described as the Angevin empire. Given the limitations of technology, communication and transport in the twelfth century, it was essential for Richard to operate, like his forebears, as an itinerant monarch, moving through his various and extensive domains almost constantly, in order to manifest his will and counter the centrifugal forces that otherwise threatened to rip his empire apart.

On these grounds, it would be wrong simply to judge Richard on the amount of time he physically spent in England. He often was forced to direct his attention across the Channel and to rule his English lands from a distance through intermediaries. This helps, in particular, to explain the Lionheart's actions in the second half of his reign, after 1194, when much of his energy was devoted to fighting a protracted territorial war on the continent against his increasingly aggressive Capetian rival, King Philip of France. During the earlier part of his reign, however, Richard's prolonged absence was prompted by events on the wider international stage: the crushing defeat of Latin forces in the Holy Land in 1187; the Muslim reconquest of Jerusalem that followed; and the clarion call to arms then broadcast throughout the West for what has come to be known as the Third Crusade.

From 1187 onwards, through to his coronation and beyond, Richard I's career was intimately intertwined with these events and this holy war. Once anointed as King of England in early September 1189, almost all of the Lionheart's initiative, energy and purpose were devoted to the planning, preparation and prosecution of the Third Crusade. But why did this newly crowned monarch – who had fought with his every fibre for the right to rule over the Angevin realm, and was already embroiled in a rancorous rivalry with the neighbouring Capetians – devote himself to such a distant conflict and a campaign that would be waged on the other side of the known world, some two thousand miles away, in Palestine?

The Near East might have been remote in geographical terms, but to medieval Christians living in Western Europe it was also a region imbued with a profound, sacred significance, being the land in which Christ himself had lived and died. The reversals of fortune endured there in 1187, at the hands of Sultan Saladin, were regarded as unprecedented cataclysms – disasters that shocked and appalled the Latin West. Close to a century earlier, the armies of the First Crusade marched from Europe to reclaim the Holy Land from Islam and enjoyed remarkable success. Jerusalem was conquered in 1099 and a series of Latin (or Frankish) settlements in the Levant – the crusader states – established.* These victories were presented as nothing less than miraculous. Behind the crusaders' achievements, it was argued, could be seen the hand of God himself. Through the early twelfth century, a deeply rooted and, it would seem, authentic sense took hold: the work of conquering and defending the Holy Land enjoyed a divine mandate; and fighting in this struggle would actually help to cleanse a Christian's soul of the taint of sin, easing his path into Heaven. Given that the contemporary vision of Christianity projected by the Latin Church emphasized the

---

* Contemporaries often described the European settlers in the Levant as 'Franks' (*Ifranj* in Arabic) because many of them originated in *Francia* (France).

perils of transgression, the imminence of Judgement and the torments of Hell, it perhaps was not surprising that, for many, crusading possessed a potent appeal.

So it was that, when the pope issued a new call to crusade in the autumn of 1187, exhorting Christians to avenge the 'crimes' committed by the supposedly demonic Saladin, many responded with ardent enthusiasm. Contemporaries reported that in November that same year Richard the Lionheart became the first nobleman north of the Alps to enlist.[3] This in itself was a remarkable decision, as up to this moment Richard had appeared to be entirely consumed by the intricacies of regional power politics – striving to ensure his succession to the English crown and the wider Angevin realm. But the allure of the crusade soon became clear, as an almost feverish surge of enthusiasm took hold in the West. An array of European nobles followed the Lionheart's lead and, within a few months, even his father, King Henry II, and Philip Augustus of France had enrolled, along with the great elder statesman of the day, the German emperor, Frederick Barbarossa. None the less, Richard's decision to take the cross, and then actually follow through by departing for a protracted campaign in Palestine at the very start of his reign, had far-reaching consequences for the kingdom of England. So, should his actions be regarded as ill-advised, even neglectful, or did he have no choice but to wage this holy war?

A range of factors suggests that Richard's commitment to the crusade was all but inevitable. Research has shown that individuals with relatives who had crusaded in the past were far more likely to do so themselves, and there can be little doubt that enthusiasm and recruitment for these holy wars were closely linked to networks of kinship and patronage.[4] Richard's own 'crusading pedigree' was clear. His mother, Queen Eleanor, had travelled to the Levant with the Second Crusade in the late 1140s, while his father, Henry II, and elder brother, Henry the Young King, had both taken the cross (though their vows were never fulfilled). The Lionheart's familial and seigneurial ties to the kingdom of Jerusalem's ruling elite were also significant. He was the great-grandson of Fulk of Anjou, King of Jerusalem (1131–42), the cousin of the current queen, Sibylla, and former feudal overlord to her husband, the Poitevin King Guy. With this kind of background, it would have been virtually impossible for Richard to ignore events in the Holy Land.

In recent decades, modern scholarship has also tended to emphasize the importance of religious fervour in crusader motivation. For most aspiring crusaders, spiritual devotion seems to have been far more potent as a stimulus than any desire for material gain or territorial acquisition. In the Lionheart's case, however, it is hard to gauge the extent to which his actions were driven by Christian piety. The surviving sources afford only fleeting glimpses of Richard as a man of faith. Like any 'good' medieval Christian nobleman, he made charitable donations to religious institutions and was a particular devotee of the ninth-century martyr Saint Edmund, an East Anglian king believed to have died resisting Viking invaders. But the Lionheart's track record in this regard suggests a depth of religiosity that might be characterized as conventional – he was no aspiring saint and far from being monkish in his habits or appetites.

None the less, one striking episode suggests that, in common with many of his contemporaries, Richard did harbour a gnawing fear of damnation. While actually en route to the Near East in the autumn of 1190, he stopped off in Sicily and there, in the chapel of an Angevin supporter named Reginald de Moac, made an animated display of contrition. Richard is said to have stripped naked, thrown himself at the feet of the assembled clergy and offered up an impassioned confession of his many sins. Around the same time, he visited a renowned southern Italian mystic and prophet, Joachim of Fiore, who confidently predicted the Lionheart's success in the coming holy war, cast Saladin as a precursor of the Anti-Christ and presented the crusade as part of a cycle of events leading towards the End of Days.[5] All of this suggests that, by late 1190 at least, Richard's thinking may have been coloured by notions of predestination and apocalypticism.

The majority of crusaders seem to have been particularly inspired by the notion that their campaign was akin to a form of pilgrimage – a sacred journey that would culminate in a visit to the most hallowed city on Earth, Jerusalem. However, the Third Crusade ended in stalemate in September 1192, with Saladin still in possession of the Holy City. Even so, the sultan rather graciously granted the crusaders access to Jerusalem if they came as unarmed pilgrims, and many availed themselves of this rare opportunity to venerate key shrines, such as the Holy Sepulchre. King Richard did not. He remained encamped on the coast of Palestine, preparing for his return journey to the West. Some have taken this as a sign that the Lionheart was not moved by a genuine sense of pious devotion, but this is too blunt a verdict. Richard had been struggling since mid August that year with a severe illness that left him fevered and bedridden, so it may well be that he was actually physically incapable of making the journey inland. It is also likely that, for a king who had failed in his quest to reconquer the Holy City, the prospect of travelling to Jerusalem, bereft of arms, in the guise of a supplicant, was simply too humiliating to entertain.

It is perhaps impossible to gauge the precise extent to which Richard regarded the crusade as an expression of Christian devotion, but there were other forces that would have made it almost inconceivable for him to ignore the pope's call to arms. At a number of levels, the Lionheart's behaviour may have been informed, or even conditioned, by societal pressures and expectations. In the course of the twelfth century it became customary for Western European kings to participate in crusades, providing leadership, financial resources and manpower. The standard was set, in 1147, when both Louis VII of France and Conrad III of Germany embarked on the ill-fated Second Crusade, hoping to defend the Holy Land. By the 1180s, Latin monarchs were all but obliged, as part of their sacred duty as God's anointed rulers on Earth, to lend their support to the cause of the holy war. Once Richard became King of England, this responsibility settled upon his shoulders. This in itself might have been enough to force his hand, but he also was living through the period in which the ideals of chivalry were beginning to exert a palpable, even prevailing, influence over the conduct of Western Europe's ruling nobility.

To speak of chivalry as a formal code of practice in the 1180s would be misleading. It was still evolving as an idea and, as yet, lacked strict or universal parameters. Even so, there was already a widely held sense that the behaviour of the knightly warrior class ought to be controlled – conditioned by a range of mutually accepted expectations – and that the greatest knights deserved to be lauded within aristocratic society as the 'best of men', or what contemporaries would have called *preudhommes*. Martial prowess, bravery and loyalty were all revered as qualities, and the leaders of knights, be they lords or kings, were also expected to display a significant degree of generosity, or largesse, to their followers. The public display of these virtues could earn an individual honour and renown, but equally transgression – whether in the form of cowardice, defeat or infidelity – would bring shame and social reprobation.

The deepening obsession with chivalric virtue coloured contemporary aristocratic culture by the time Richard I ascended the throne, and the pursuit of honour and renown seem to have featured heavily in his own thinking about the Third Crusade. Clergymen may have promoted this holy war as a pathway to spiritual redemption, but within lay society it was also popularized as a glorious endeavour that could earn participants unparalleled fame – an expedition, akin to the greatest tournament on Earth, in which warriors could prove their worth against Saladin and his Muslim horde. Failure to participate in such a monumental venture would be the cause of shame. Around this time, one of Richard's contemporaries – the French knight and Third Crusader Conon of Béthune – composed an Old French verse avowing these sentiments. 'Now we will see who will be truly brave,' he wrote, '[and] if we permit our mortal enemies to stay [in the Holy Land] our lives will be shameful for evermore.' Conon also declared that any who are 'healthy, young and rich cannot remain behind without suffering shame'. As enthusiasm for the war swept across Western Europe, men who did not join the crusade were exposed to accusations of cowardice and publicly humiliated by receiving gifts of 'wool and distaff' (the tools for spinning), to intimate that they were fit only for women's work – the medieval equivalent of the white feather.[6]

Richard himself was not immune to this type of vocal criticism. At first he was praised for the speed with which he committed to the crusade. In 1188, the southern French knight and troubadour Bertrand of Born penned a verse declaring that Richard, 'the one who is count and duke and will be king, has stepped forward, which doubles his renown, for he loves renown more than anyone of the two religions, the Christians and the unbaptized'. But a year and a half later, when the departure of the main Angevin and Capetian armies on crusade continued to be delayed by protracted succession disputes and bitter wrangling between the Lionheart and Philip Augustus, Bertrand's tone soured markedly. 'I know of two kings who hold back,' he declared. 'King Philip is one, because he fears King Richard, who in turn fears him. Would they were both now in Sir Saladin's chains, for they are cheating God: they have taken the cross and do nothing about leaving.'[7]

The devotional allure of the holy war, when combined with Richard's own crusading pedigree, and the compelling forces of social expectation and chivalric obligation, meant that the Lionheart's participation in the Third Crusade was essentially unavoidable. It would have been unthinkable for him to turn his back on the war in Palestine once he became king. Nevertheless, the depth of his commitment to the cause – the steadfast pursuit of the Holy Land's recovery – was not a given. His rival and contemporary, King Philip of France, also felt the inescapable pull of the crusade. Like Richard, Philip led an army to the Near East, arriving at the great siege of Acre in April 1191. But his approach to the conflict was more limited and pragmatic. Once Acre was reconquered in early July, Philip immediately announced his intention to return to Europe. He had achieved a degree of success in the Levant, but the more pressing business of defending and expanding the interests of the Capetian realm in France demanded his attention. Many contemporaries considered this a betrayal, with one crusader later pointedly writing: 'God's mercy! What a turnaround!'[8] Yet, at one level, Philip was merely prioritizing his role as a monarch above that of a crusader – putting the needs of his kingdom first. Arguably, Richard could have followed this lead.

At the other end of the spectrum, however, were kings whose staunch dedication to the crusading cause was near-absolute. Somewhat ironically, the prime example in this case was Philip Augustus's own grandson, King Louis IX of France. He fought on two crusades in the mid thirteenth century: the first saw him absent himself from Europe for close to six years, and precipitated a period of significant instability in France; the second culminated in his death in north Africa. Louis IX may eventually have been canonized as a saint in recognition of his devotion to the holy war, but there can be little doubt that, in pursuit of victory in the East, he neglected his duties at home.

Richard I's behaviour placed him somewhere between these two extremes. Though he never truly turned his back on the kingdom of England, or the Angevin realm as a whole, he was clearly captivated by the prospect of leading the Third Crusade on to a successful conclusion, and thus proved willing to dedicate the early years of his reign to this cause. His motives may well have had more to do with the secular rewards of this endeavour than any supposed spiritual benefits. This is not to suggest that he sought wealth or territory in the Levant, but rather that he craved the unprecedented fame and glory offered by the holy war. A fundamental feature of Richard's life that shaped much of his behaviour is that he thought of himself not only as a nobleman, duke or king, but also as a knight. This meant that he aspired to achieve greatness both as a monarch, ruling over a powerful realm, and as a chivalric warrior earning renown in battle. And the Lionheart's ambitions were not confined to his English realm, or even to the broader territories of the Angevin empire: his sights were set on the wider world and the international arena.

All of this begs the question: did Richard carelessly exploit England's resources in pursuit of crusading victory? In fact, his actions during the first year of his reign suggest that two interlocking objectives were prioritized:

gathering the financial means with which to fund the holy war; but also ensuring the kingdom's security in his absence. Though new to the throne, the Lionheart already had some experience of war and clearly understood that military campaigns were not won through bravery and prowess alone. In the Middle Ages, as in any era, successful armies needed resources – from weapons and armour to horses, ships and above all food. These essentials cost money, and the sheer scale of the coming expedition meant that it would be more expensive than most.

From the moment he came to power, Richard set his sights on amassing the largest possible war chest. Some significant progress had already been made in this regard by his father. In 1188, Henry II had instituted the so-called Saladin Tithe – a levy of 10 per cent on all movable goods, enforced by threat of excommunication – and though this tax proved hugely unpopular, it nevertheless brought in the vast sum of 100,000 marks. Collections continued under the new king, but Richard also looked to broaden and intensify the crown's money-raising efforts by auctioning off lands, titles and privileges. According to one eyewitness, in England 'he put up for sale all he had – offices, lordships, earldoms, sheriffdoms, castles, towns, everything'. Indeed, the Lionheart was supposed to have joked that he would have sold London if he could.[9]

In reality, Richard's approach does not seem to have been quite so reckless. It was the case, for example, that he replaced all but five of the twenty-seven sheriffs in post in England at the end of Henry II's reign, with each new sheriff having to pay the crown a handsome 'fine' in return for this valuable honour. But recent research has concluded that these appointments were made with 'prudence and foresight', as candidates were carefully vetted for their prospective administrative efficiency and loyalty to the king.[10] The measures adopted by Richard at the start of his reign also helped to shape English history by setting many of the realm's most important urban settlements on the path to prosperity. On 18 November 1189, the burgesses of Northampton were granted a measure of self-governance and freedom from tolls in exchange for the payment of £120, while a few weeks later the members of the merchant guild in the cathedral city of Bath purchased the right to hold their own markets.

All told, Richard's efforts to increase royal revenue proved remarkably successful. In the first accounting year of the Lionheart's reign, the crown amassed more than £31,000 – double the income recorded from the preceding twelve months. This reservoir of wealth enabled Richard to dominate and direct the Third Crusade, in part because his financial resources far surpassed those possessed by Philip of France. The Lionheart also spent around £14,000 preparing for the expedition: readying transport and shipping; stockpiling essential supplies. This included the purchase of at least 60,000 horseshoes and some 14,000 cured pigs' carcasses.

Through all of these measures, however, Richard did not go so far as to strip England of its resources and defences; nor could his approach to the governance of the realm be fairly described as negligent. In fact, he was at pains to prepare the kingdom for the prolonged period of royal absence demanded by the crusade and introduced a series of measures designed to preserve stability and security. There can be no doubt that, although the Lionheart craved victory in the East, he was also determined to return home to a realm that remained intact.

One of Richard's first priorities was to ensure that he retained the support of a well-ordered Church in England. A critical step in this regard was resolving the feud between Baldwin, Archbishop of Canterbury, and the Benedictine monks of Canterbury's cathedral priory. This heated dispute had long sapped the energy and attention of the kingdom's leading churchmen, but by taking a personal role in negotiations, Richard deftly orchestrated a swift reconciliation in the autumn of 1189. He also moved to fill a range of prominent ecclesiastical offices left vacant by his father – including the sees of London, Winchester and Worcester – thus helping to ensure the Church's efficient governance and its continued loyalty to the crown.

Ecclesiastical affairs also impacted upon another obvious area of concern: the potential for disloyalty by members of Richard's family during his absence. The ambitions of Henry II's bastard son Geoffrey were duly quietened by his appointment as Archbishop of York. However, the question of the Lionheart's younger brother, John, was not so readily resolved. Now in his early twenties, John had acquired a well-earned reputation for duplicity and possessed few redeeming qualities in terms of character or capability. Having lived the life of the youngest son – a landless and stunted princeling, ever in the shadow of his greater forebears – John made for an unreliable ally and would become an open threat. Where their father, Henry II, had sought to keep John in check by depriving him of lands and wealth, Richard opted to feed his sibling's appetite for power until it was sated. John's rights to the county of Mortain in Normandy were confirmed, and he also received lands in west and south-west England, as well as control of the major crown fortress at Marlborough. In England alone, he stood to receive an annual income of £4,000, but in return he was required to swear an oath that he would remain on the continent and not set foot in the kingdom for three years – a sure sign that Richard harboured deep misgivings about his brother's fidelity.

To counter any threat to his position and the crown's authority during his absence, Richard also instituted an innovative and largely effective system of administration. It was customary for kings of England to deputize a representative, or justiciar, to wield power in their stead when outside the realm. Richard appointed his Norman-born chancellor, William Longchamp, to this office (while also making him Bishop of Ely, guardian of the Tower of London and keeper of the royal seal), but to ensure that the fate of the realm did not lie in the hands of just one man, four so-called 'co-justiciars' were selected – trusted nobles, tasked with supervising the management of the kingdom. In addition, Richard looked to rely upon the sage counsel and steadying hand offered by his mother, Queen Eleanor, who would oversee affairs of state in England and the wider Angevin world for the duration of the Third Crusade. At the same time, he planned to maintain a channel of communication with his European domains through the regular exchange of letters.

Richard also looked to shore up the defences of England's borders in advance of his departure to the Levant. To the north, peace was secured with William the Lion, King of Scotland, by the restoration of a number of frontier castles previously confiscated by Henry II. In the west, along the Welsh march, the Lionheart installed the formidable knight William Marshal – a warrior of proven quality, with a record of staunch loyalty to the crown – as lord of Chepstow Castle. Marshal was also to serve as one of the four co-justiciars. But as ever, the thorniest issue, eclipsing even the danger presented by John, was the looming threat posed by Richard's neighbour and rival, Philip of France. Richard could be sure that, were he to make a hurried departure for the East, the Capetian monarch would seek to capitalize upon his absence, making mischief at every turn and threatening to seize contested territory in regions such as Normandy and Berry. The only solution was to orchestrate a simultaneous departure. After a succession of planning meetings held on 30 December 1189 and on 16 March and 2 July 1190, all of the complex preparations were finalized. At last, on 4 July 1190 – the third anniversary of the terrible disaster at Hattin – the main Angevin and Capetian armies set out from Vézelay to wage the Third Crusade.

On the whole, Richard's precautions proved to be broadly effective, but problems arose with his choice for the office of chief justiciar, William Longchamp. Though unquestionably loyal to the king, Longchamp's brusque and overbearing manner soon alienated much of the remaining English court. By late 1190, the group of co-justiciars had seen fit to despatch a letter complaining about Long-champ's conduct, and this duly reached the Lionheart in February 1191 on the island of Sicily, where he was waiting for the sea lanes to open with the end of winter. Richard responded by sending the trusted prelate Archbishop Wal-ter of Rouen back to England with a pair of royal writs authorizing him to depose Longchamp should the need arise. The embattled justiciar remained in post until Octo-ber 1191, but was eventually stripped of his powers and fled into exile in Flanders. According to one particularly lurid account of these events, Longchamp tried to evade imprisonment by disguising himself as a woman, but this scheme supposedly misfired when, while waiting for a ship on the coast near Dover, he was accosted by an amorous fisherman and ended up being chased down the beach.[11]

At the same time, John sought to capitalize upon his brother's absence on crusade. The promise not to visit Eng-land was broken in 1191, as John pressed his claims to be recognized as Richard's formally designated heir and led the calls for Longchamp's deposition. By that autumn, his role as 'supreme governor of the realm' – in essence the regent – had been acknowledged by England's leading nobles, and he was also permitted to assume control of a clutch of royal castles.[12] But John's independence was still curtailed by Queen Eleanor and Archbishop Walter of Rouen, who had replaced Longchamp as chief justiciar. Once Philip had returned to Europe in December 1191, John seems to have considered the idea of forming a direct alliance with the Capetians, but he soon relented when Eleanor threatened to confiscate all of his English lands and strongholds if he crossed the Channel to meet the French king.

In fact, it was only after the end of the crusade and King Richard's capture in Austria that the system of checks and balances began to crumble, leaving England and the wider Angevin territories exposed. On these grounds, it might be fairly concluded that Richard made the best of an intractable situation when seeking to balance his desire (and perhaps need) to prosecute a sustained crusading campaign in the Near East against the necessity of defending his kingdom at home. Even so, the Lionheart perhaps was guilty of one major failing when it came to ensuring the future security of the realm: the provision of an heir and successor.

The issue of royal succession weighed heavily upon the minds of most medieval monarchs. England's tangled history through the course of the eleventh and twelfth centuries attested to the grave disorder that might result from the contested transfer of power. When Edward the Confessor died childless in 1066, he left the door open to the Norman Conquest, while the accidental drowning of Henry I's only son in 1120 precipitated the dreadful anarchy of King Stephen's reign. It seems to have been Henry II's deep concern with the question of succession that prompted him to take the unusual step of crowning his eldest son, Young Henry, as co-ruler in 1170. On the face of it, Richard by contrast appeared to have an almost cavalier attitude to the essential question of who might succeed him as ruler of England and the broader Angevin realm. Even as he departed for the Holy Land, the matter lay open to debate, with the Lionheart seemingly poised between two potential candidates – his brother John, or his young nephew Arthur of Brittany (the son of Richard's late brother Geoffrey).

King Richard was only in his early thirties, but even so he knew full well that a sudden and untimely death remained a possibility. In 1183, a bout of dysentery had taken his eldest brother, Henry, from good health to his deathbed in mere weeks, while his brother Geoffrey of Brittany was killed three years later when he fell from his horse during a knightly tournament in France. The Third Crusade also proved to be an extraordinarily lethal campaign, from which Richard was lucky to emerge alive.

Why then did this monarch – otherwise so assiduous in matters of war and governance – lack a clear heir? In the mid twentieth century, some scholars popularized the notion that Richard's failure to produce a successor was a consequence of his homosexuality. This idea was based in large part on a single medieval chronicler's report that the Lionheart had shared a bed with Philip Augustus in the summer of 1187, while they were plotting Henry II's downfall. But as one prominent academic historian has since pointed out, this encounter cannot be judged by modern standards and should rather be interpreted as a 'political gesture of peace or alliance, not erotic passion'.[13]

In fact, Richard actually acquired a somewhat unsavoury reputation among contemporaries as a predatory womanizer. In the early 1180s, he was said to have abused his position as Duke of Aquitaine by abducting 'his subjects' wives, daughters and kinswomen', forcing them to serve as his concubines. Towards the end of his reign, Richard was also rumoured to have become infatuated with a nun at Fontevraud Abbey. Much of the tale of this prospective liaison, as it was later told, seems barely credible – on learning that the Lionheart was particularly taken with her captivating eyes, the nun was supposed to have plucked them out and sent them to the king in defiance – but the story was obviously grounded in the belief that Richard had heterosexual, not homosexual, appetites. This same belief was reflected in one early thirteenth-century chronicler's assertion that the Lionheart probably would have survived the wound that killed him in 1199 if only he had followed his surgeon's orders and abstained from bedding whores.[14]

It remains possible that Richard was bisexual, of course, but the question of his precise sexual orientation hardly matters – the point is that his tastes did not prevent him from siring an heir. The notion that the Lionheart might have been infertile can also be discarded, given that he is known to have fathered at least one illegitimate son, Philip of Cognac. The real issue seems to have been neither desire, nor capacity, but the securing of a suitable wife. Richard originally was betrothed to King Louis VII's daughter, Alice of France, in 1169 as part of a plan to secure peace between the Angevin and Capetian dynasties. Thereafter, Alice resided within the Angevin court, but her union with the Lionheart was never concluded, and Richard showed little interest in her, perhaps in part because she was widely rumoured to have become Henry II's mistress.

In the end, Richard settled on a bride just as he was embarking on the Third Crusade: the Iberian princess Berengaria of Navarre. This was a politically expedient match, orchestrated in the main by Queen Eleanor, that secured the duchy of Aquitaine's southern border during Richard's absence. The Queen Mother chaperoned Berengaria on her journey to meet her new husband at Messina, on the island of Sicily, in early 1191, though their marriage was not formally enacted until they reached Cyprus. Berengaria then accompanied Richard on his journey to the Holy Land, but from this point onwards the couple had little contact. Though their union remained intact – probably in large part because the Lionheart could ill afford to alienate his Navarrese allies – it produced no children and it may be that Berengaria was barren.

Though Richard's hands may have been partially tied, his failure to adequately address the issue of succession must be recognized as a significant blemish on his record. Of course, he could not have foreseen the exact circumstances of his sudden demise in 1199, but even so, his attitude towards the urgent matter of furnishing his realm with a legitimate heir seems unusually relaxed. For most medieval kings this was a primary obsession – an issue pursued almost regardless of the cost. In Richard's case, however, the choice between John and Arthur remained largely unresolved until the Lionheart lay on his deathbed. Only then was Richard said to have finally confirmed his younger brother as his heir: a decision that would have catastrophic consequences for England and the entire Angevin realm.

1. King Richard I, shown here in an illustration from a mid-thirteenth-century chronicle by Matthew Paris, succeeded to the English throne in 1189.

2. The reverse of Richard's royal seal from 1198, depicting 'the Lionheart', as he was already known in his lifetime, as a mounted knight, his shield bearing the three-lions device that would be adopted as the royal coat of arms in England.

3. Richard enlisted in the Third Crusade in 1187, even before he became king, after the Muslim sultan Saladin (depicted above) reconquered the city of Jerusalem for Islam. Richard and Saladin became arch rivals in the war for the Holy Land.

4 and 5. Fighting alongside Philip II of France, Richard swiftly concluded the great siege of Acre. Left, the two monarchs (Philip in blue) are shown receiving Acre's surrender on 12 July 1191. When negotiations for the release of the city's Muslim garrison broke down, Richard had some 2,700 captives executed (below).

6. On 7 September 1191, Richard was confronted by the full might of Saladin's forces in the Battle of Arsuf and, as this nineteenth-century engraving suggests, the Lionheart fought in the thick of the fray.

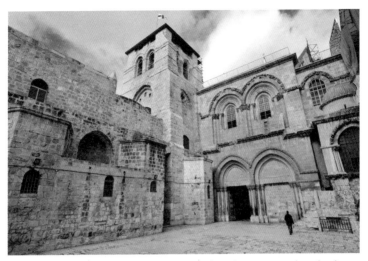

7. Richard made two advances on Jerusalem, but retreated on both occasions without ever laying siege to the city. As a result, the Third Crusade ended with Christendom's most sacred site – the Church of the Holy Sepulchre (above) – still in Muslim hands.

8. These mid-thirteenth-century tiles, discovered in Chertsey Abbey, Surrey, depict Richard triumphing over Saladin in single combat, reflecting how the Lionheart's achievements were widely mythologized in the later Middle Ages.

9. Between 1196 and 1198, Richard spent a fortune constructing this mighty castle – Château Gaillard – perched above the River Seine, but it enabled him to neutralize the threat posed by Philip II and thus reclaim the duchy of Normandy.

10. Mortally wounded by a crossbow bolt during a minor siege, Richard died on 6 April 1199 and was laid to rest beside his father, Henry II, in Fontevraud Abbey, where the Lionheart's tomb effigy can still be seen today.

fighting march south along the coast to Jaffa in the late summer of 1191, even as Saladin strove to stop him in his tracks. From this point onwards, however, progress faltered. In the months that followed, the Lionheart made not just one, but two failed attempts to march inland towards Jerusalem, yet on both occasions he elected to retreat without ever launching a direct assault or initiating a siege. In September 1192, the crusade ended in stalemate. Richard had conquered a valuable strip of coastal territory, breathing new life into the crusader states, but fell short of achieving the expedition's primary objective – the Holy City's reconquest. Given the campaign's indecisive outcome, it is reasonable to ask whether the Lionheart deserves his well-established reputation as one of Western Europe's greatest crusade leaders. Was Richard in fact to blame for the Third Crusade's limited achievements? And could he actually have led the Latin armies to outright victory?

In assessing Richard I's crusading career, the extent of his ambitions for the expedition must first be acknowledged. Rather than simply focusing upon the Holy Land, the Lionheart seems to have envisioned his campaign to the Near East as one component of a broader strategy to deal with dynastic affairs and assert Angevin influence in the Mediterranean. Having decided to journey to the Levant via ship rather than overland, Richard plotted a course that conveniently brought him from Marseilles south along the Italian coast to the island kingdom of Sicily in late September 1190. Thirteen years earlier, King Henry II's interest in international affairs had prompted him to marry off his young daughter Joanne to Sicily's ruling sovereign,

William II. But William had died in November 1189, prompting a succession crisis that saw the late king's illegitimate cousin, Tancred of Lecce – an ambitious schemer of dwarf-like stature – seize power and take Joanne prisoner. Upon his arrival, Richard used a mixture of direct military aggression and insistent negotiation to secure not only Joanne's release, but also a payment of 40,000 ounces of gold (partly in recompense for his sister Joanne's previously withheld dower). Before departing, the Lionheart also secured a prospective marriage alliance between his three-year-old nephew Arthur of Brittany and one of Tancred's daughters.

With the coming of spring, the sea lanes reopened, and Richard set sail on 10 April 1191, apparently with the intent of travelling on to Palestine as quickly as possible. In the event, he seized control of the Byzantine-held island of Cyprus before he ever set foot in the Holy Land. The supposed course of events that culminated in this providential conquest seems a little too propitious to be entirely accidental: the onset of a sudden storm dividing the Lionheart's fleet, leaving three of his ships wrecked off the Cypriot coast; the ill-treatment meted out to their crews by the local populace offering Richard a ready cause to launch an armed intervention. Perhaps there was an element of premeditation behind the Lionheart's actions – indeed, it may even be that he had always intended to make landfall on Cyprus, storm or no. As it was, Richard was able to brand the island's Greek Christian ruler, Isaac Comnenus, a 'tyrant' and effect a swift military coup.[1] The initial intention seems to have been to establish an Angevin outpost on

Cyprus, and two English knights were installed as governors. Once the Lionheart and his great crusading army departed, however, insurrection soon broke out on the island. With his mind now more firmly focused on events in Palestine, Richard elected to sell Cyprus to the Templars for the price of 100,000 gold bezants, although admittedly he only ever received the initial down-payment of 40,000. The island would remain in Latin hands for almost four hundred years and served as an important staging post in the war for the Holy Land.

From an Angevin perspective, then, Richard's Mediterranean adventure proved to be an enormous success even before his battle against Saladin began in earnest. There also can be no doubt that Richard's military contribution transformed the fortunes of the Third Crusade once he reached the mainland. In part this was because the Lionheart brought his own, not inconsiderable, martial expertise to bear. His knowledge of war – and, in particular, the harsh realities of medieval siege-craft – had been cultivated through long years of governing the unruly duchy of Aquitaine and contesting the course of the Angevin succession. An aura of mystique had already begun to settle around Richard, linked to his vaunted prowess in combat and impetuous bravery.

Richard also arrived in the Levant at the head of a sizeable, well-resourced and disciplined army. As ever when dealing with medieval warfare, precise figures are virtually impossible to recover, but one contemporary estimate suggests that the Lionheart left Sicily with 17,000 troops and, by the standards of the day, the Angevin fleet of some 200 vessels was enormous. In contrast, Philip Augustus's force seems to have contained just 650 knights and 1,300 squires, and the French king arrived in Palestine with a mere six ships.

The strict rules governing conduct within the Angevin fleet give some indication of King Richard's authoritarian approach to command. Among a long list of harsh penalties for disorder was the provision that 'Whoever shall slay a man while on a ship shall be bound to the corpse and thrown into the sea. If he shall slay him on land, he shall be bound to the corpse and buried [alive] in the earth.'[2] Richard's assiduous preparations for the crusade meant that his men would be equipped with all the necessary materials of war, from arms and armour to crossbow bolts and horseshoes. Furthermore, the king used his time in Sicily to amass a supply of hefty catapult stones and to construct a sophisticated wooden siege tower, known as Mategriffon, that could be broken down into sections, transported by ship and then reassembled in the Holy Land.

Richard also had the deep financial resources required to fund a victorious campaign. The successful implementation of the Saladin Tithe, alongside the Lionheart's own extensive money-raising efforts, had filled the Angevin war chest, while the recent success in Cyprus only added more money to the coffers. Indeed, in almost every respect, Richard I's qualities and resources outshone those of Philip Augustus, a man eight years his junior and his main rival for command of the crusade. Even their enemies were aware of the differences. Once the two kings arrived in the Levant, a Muslim contemporary observed that the French monarch was 'a great man and respected leader, one of their great kings', but added that the Lionheart 'had much experience of fighting and was intrepid in battle' and in comparison to 'the king of France [was] richer and more renowned for martial skill and courage'.[3]

Richard may have been well placed to emerge as the guiding force behind the Third Crusade, but he would require all of his skill and strength to overcome the challenge now set before him: defeating the fearsome Muslim sultan Saladin and reasserting Latin dominion over the Holy Land. Saladin had come to power some twenty years earlier. The son of a Kurdish warlord named Ayyub, he began by establishing a powerbase in Egypt and then, drawing upon the fabled wealth of the Nile, set about extending his influence and authority into Syria and Mesopotamia. By 1186, Saladin controlled the great cities of Damascus and Aleppo, and had even subdued Mosul on the far-flung banks of the River Tigris, ushering in an unprecedented era of Muslim unity and establishing the foundations of an enduring Ayyubid empire.

These successes were fuelled by Saladin's oft-repeated assurances that he would wage a determined jihad against the crusader states, reclaiming Palestine and the sacred city of Jerusalem for Islam. In 1187, he finally made good on his word, leading some 40,000 troops to war against the massed might of the Latin kingdom of Jerusalem. On 4 July at Hattin, in Galilee, Saladin scored a stunning victory, crushing the Christian army and capturing their king, Guy of Lusignan. In the months that followed, Muslim forces swept through Palestine, seizing key sites, including the coastal settlements of Acre and Ascalon, before finally toppling Jerusalem itself on 2 October. It was these grand triumphs that had sparked the Third Crusade and brought Richard I to the Holy Land. They also transformed Saladin into a living legend.

By the time the Lionheart reached Palestine in June 1191, Saladin was in his early fifties, his finest hour behind him. Age had begun to weaken the sultan's constitution and he suffered from frequent, debilitating bouts of ill-health. None the less, he remained a redoubtable figure: admired by his followers as a champion of the holy war; shrewd in the arenas of politics and diplomacy; cautious yet competent in the field of battle. Richard I was thirty-three when he arrived in the Near East. Though hardly a neophyte, he was relatively new to the crown and largely untested on the international stage. In Saladin he found a well-matched opponent – a foil against whom his mettle would be tested to breaking point.

The first martial challenge to confront King Richard upon his arrival in the Levant was breaking the grim deadlock at the great siege of Acre. This extraordinary investment had begun almost two years earlier. The port city of Acre, in the northern reaches of the kingdom of Jerusalem, fell to Saladin in the immediate aftermath of the Battle of Hattin. By the summer of 1189, however, King Guy had been released from Muslim captivity and decided to make a seemingly suicidal attempt to reconquer the fortified settlement. Guy marched south along the Mediterranean coast at the head of perhaps 2,000 troops and laid siege to Acre on 28 August.

At first, this offensive seemed like utter madness. It ran counter to every custom of medieval warfare, because under normal circumstances any attempt to assault a stronghold deep in enemy territory would end in catastrophe. In theory, all the opposition had to do was bring up a field army, encircle the besiegers and either starve them into submission or crush them to a pulp. But in 1189 Guy's determined Latin army dug in, creating a network of well-defended trenches around Acre. Their position on the coast also meant that the sea could act as a vital conduit of supply and reinforcement. When Saladin deployed his army in support of the Muslim garrison inside Acre, he proved unable to overrun the Frankish positions. Any damage he could do was swiftly repaired, any troops killed or captured soon replaced by new arrivals. The siege of Acre evolved into the first military engagement of the Third Crusade, and, as the months passed, both sides found themselves caught in a dreadful stalemate. In the face of appalling privation and near-incessant military pressure, the Latin crusaders remained resolute, simply refusing to give up their cause, but they lacked the resources to breach Acre's looming circuit of walls and overcome its garrison. For his part, Saladin maintained his counter-siege – with a field army encamped on the plains surrounding the Frankish trenches – but failed to break the investment.

The siege dragged on through two horrendous winters, with disease and hunger wreaking havoc in the Christian and Muslim camps alike, and no end in sight. Philip of France was able to restore some momentum within the crusader camp once he arrived at the head of a small fleet on 20

April 1191. Work began on the construction of seven large stone-throwing machines, and the makeshift palisade surrounding the crusaders' trenches was strengthened. In preparation for a proposed frontal assault on Acre's walls, Philip also ordered that sections of the deep dry-moat surrounding the port should be filled. This led to a rather desperate and macabre struggle, as Franks began throwing animal carcasses and even human corpses into the ditch, while parties of Muslims set about the grisly task of undoing their efforts by dismembering and removing the remains.

Progress was being made by the Christians, but the tempo of operations only really changed once the Lionheart reached Acre on 8 June. With Richard's forces in play, the crusaders could encircle the port's landward walls with some 25,000 troops and, in spite of the simmering antagonism that persisted with Philip, there was a fair measure of positive coordination and collaboration between the Angevin and Capetian contingents. The Lionheart put two exceptionally powerful stone-throwing machines into the field – engines that may well have made use of advanced counterweight technology to propel heavier missiles further and with greater accuracy. Richard's siege machines, when added to Philip's arsenal, enabled the crusaders to subject Acre to a withering, near-constant aerial barrage, supplemented by arrow and crossbow volleys. Through the month of June, these attacks weakened the port's fortifications and eroded the Muslim garrison's morale, while also providing valuable covering fire under which teams of Latin sappers could begin tunnelling beneath Acre's walls.

Some of the force of Richard I's arrival was blunted

when he fell ill with a scurvy-like affliction called *arnaldia* by contemporaries, which caused his teeth and fingernails to loosen and patches of hair to fall out. The Lionheart was confined to his tent for a number of weeks, but once he began to recover the king took to being carried to the frontline on a stretcher and used his crossbow to pick off Muslim troops on Acre's battlements. At the same time, Saladin's every attempt to overrun the crusaders' trenches was driven back. One Muslim eyewitness, based in the sultan's camp, observed that frustration at these repeated failures left Saladin overcome with 'tiredness, dejection and grief', while adding that 'the defenders in the city had become very weak and the noose around them very tight'.[4]

The end was in sight after French crusaders managed to effect a minor breach in Acre's western defences on 3 July. This small fissure proved difficult to exploit, but two days later Richard's sappers brought down a larger section of the northern battlements. The Lionheart then took the extraordinary step of offering a reward of up to four gold coins – roughly equivalent to a year's pay – to anyone brave enough to rush forward, through a torrent of Muslim arrows and crossbow bolts, and collect a stone from the damaged wall. The ploy worked, and by 11 July a substantial gap in the walls had been created. A path into the port now stood open. Despite Saladin's last-ditch attempts to rally his troops, terms of surrender were agreed, and Acre's beleaguered garrison capitulated on 12 July 1191. This victory proved to be the Third Crusade's most important and enduring success in Palestine. Though built in part on the foundations laid by King Guy and other crusaders, the real credit for driving the siege on to its conclusion lay with Philip and, perhaps above all, Richard.

With Acre back in Christian hands, Philip announced his intention to return to Europe, and the task of reconquering the rest of the Holy Land fell to the Lionheart. In military terms, the next objective was to move the campaign on from Acre by pushing south into Palestine. Had a lesser general been at the helm, this phase of the crusade might well have ended in defeat for the Franks. Saladin's prestige had been damaged by the fall of Acre, but he still commanded a large field army that was well placed to harass, hinder and most likely halt any invading force. Knowing full well that an advance would meet with stern resistance, Richard conceived of a masterful strategy that enabled the crusaders to forge a path through Muslim-held territory.

Rather than head inland – where the chances of being isolated and surrounded would increase – the Lionheart selected a coast-hugging route south, so that his army's right flank could be protected by the sea. This approach also allowed the Latin host to be shadowed by a Christian fleet carrying supplies and reinforcements. Even more importantly, Richard focused on carefully regulating the speed of his march. This would be no lightning raid where confusion and disorder might leave the crusaders exposed. Instead of racing south, the Lionheart chose to move at a deliberate pace, enabling his troops to maintain strictly controlled formations, while relying upon the strength of their armour and sheer weight of numbers to resist aerial bombardments or direct assaults by Saladin's troops. The plan was audacious and immensely risky. Should any crusaders break ranks – whether through fear, exhaustion or simple accident – the whole army might be exposed and readily overrun. Iron-fast discipline was the key, and it fell to the Lionheart to hold his troops in place. Marching in their midst, his vast banner visible for all to see, Richard aimed to be a constant, reassuring presence; drawing upon his own bloody-minded force of will, charisma as a leader and burgeoning martial reputation to inspire his men and compel obedience.

The crusaders left Acre on 22 August 1191. For the next two weeks, they inched their way southwards, while Saladin launched repeated skirmishing attacks, hoping to break open the Frankish lines. Muslim archers and crossbowmen peppered the Christian ranks with arrows and quarrels and yet they held firm. There were casualties, and even King Richard himself was struck by a missile on 3 September, though his armour saved him from injury, but nothing could halt the crusaders' inexorable advance. On 7 September, with the Latins fast approaching the relative safety of the port at Jaffa, Saladin made a desperate attempt to stop them in their tracks. Drawing up the full weight of his field army on the plains of Arsuf, numbering perhaps 30,000 troops, the sultan tried to lure the Lionheart into a pitched battle.

The Western Christian eyewitness and crusader Ambroise – who composed a highly influential Old French account of the expedition, favouring Richard – argued that the Angevin king had always planned to face Saladin at Arsuf, and in the modern era most historians have followed this lead, maintaining that the Lionheart deliberately chose to seek battle on 7 September. Much has been made of this encounter, with one scholar even describing it as 'the last great triumph of the Christians in the Near East'. The clash at Arsuf would turn out to be the only direct military confrontation between Saladin and the Lionheart, but the battle may not have been all that it seems. Ambroise's version of events was written in the aftermath of the crusade, in full knowledge of the fact that Richard failed to reconquer Jerusalem. Hungry for opportunities to present his hero as a triumphant commander, the author seems to have deliberately sculpted a heightened account of the events at Arsuf, hoping to highlight this moment of untrammelled success. Other pieces of evidence, including the king's own letters and eyewitness Arabic chronicles, suggest that the Franks were actually drawn into battle almost by accident and paint the Lionheart's generalship as reactive rather than proactive.[5]

In reality, Richard's first priority on 7 September seems to have been to continue forging a path southwards by maintaining the forward momentum of the crusaders' fighting march. On this occasion, however, troop discipline in the army's rearguard finally faltered. Facing unbearable pressure – with baying Muslim skirmishers racing forward and the sky darkened by a murderous hail of arrows – two Christian knights, humiliated by their enforced inaction, suddenly broke ranks and rode at full tilt towards the enemy. As the Lionheart looked back from his position in the centre of the army, large swathes of the rearguard and crusader left flank followed their lead.

Richard may not have sought a battle, but one was now upon him.

Hesitation would have heralded disaster, but the Angevin king sprang into immediate action. Wheeling his horse, he led the remainder of his mounted troops in support of the crusader charge. This force had mown a devastating path across the plains of Arsuf, but – with its momentum spent – now stood to face the full brunt of a deadly Muslim counter-attack. The Lionheart's arrival helped to repel this assault. One Latin eyewitness depicted the king's fearsome martial prowess in epic terms, reporting that Richard's 'sword cleared a wide path on all sides . . . [cutting] down that unspeakable race . . . so that the corpses of the [enemy] covered the ground everywhere for the space of half a mile'.[6]

This may well have been a gross exaggeration, but Richard does seem to have played a central role in salvaging a partial victory for the crusaders at Arsuf. Saladin recognized that his chance to crush an isolated portion of the Latin army had passed, and hastily initiated a somewhat chastening retreat. Estimates suggest that he lost 32 emirs and a further 700 troops – a significant blow, but hardly crippling. The crusaders were able to regroup and continue their march, arriving at Jaffa on 10 September. In the past, historians have suggested that the Battle of Arsuf was the most important military encounter of the Third Crusade, and perhaps even of the Lionheart's entire career. One prominent scholar described the victory as marking the 'height of Richard's fame', while praising the king's generalship as 'masterful'.[7] In fact, the outcome of Arsuf was far from decisive. This reversal, when combined with the humiliation of Acre's fall, left Saladin stung, yet unbroken.

Close to a year later, King Richard's decisive military intervention once again prevented a potentially calamitous reversal. By late July 1192, the war for the Holy Land was edging towards an inconclusive end. Neither side had been able to land a fatal blow. The crusaders retained control of a narrow strip of coastal territory, but had proved unable to conquer Jerusalem itself. As thoughts turned towards the possibility of a negotiated settlement, the Lionheart returned to Acre to ponder his next move. Perceiving an opportunity to reset the balance of power, Saladin led a sudden strike on Jaffa, the crusaders' strategically vital beachhead on the Mediterranean coast. The fortified port managed to hold out against the sultan's troops for three days, but on 31 July the outer walls were breached, and what was left of the Frankish garrison withdrew into Jaffa's makeshift citadel. As Muslim troops ranged through the streets, pillaging and plundering at will, Saladin stood on the brink of a significant victory – one that might fracture the Latins' foothold in Palestine.

At dawn the following day, however, blaring trumpets were heard, presaging the arrival of a crusader fleet. Once news of the assault on Jaffa reached Richard, he immediately sailed from Acre with a relief force and raced down the coast, arriving at the embattled port on 1 August. Facing terrible odds, the Lionheart spearheaded a daring beach assault – reportedly leaping waist-deep into the sea and wading ashore alongside a handful of his closest knights. Linking up with the remnants of Jaffa's garrison, the king managed to retake the port and Saladin withdrew his forces, supposedly 'more angry than a wolf [and] feverish with fear'.[8]

Richard's troops were still dangerously exposed and heavily outnumbered. He established a camp outside Jaffa and set to work hurriedly repairing the town's defences, but by 5 August Saladin was ready to launch a renewed assault. The Lionheart and his small force of indomitable crusaders demonstrated their remarkable bravery and skill at arms that day, repelling wave after wave of attack. A Christian chronicler likened their survival to 'a great miracle at which all the world wonders', and Arabic sources confirm that the hard-pressed Franks fought with remarkable ferocity. A member of Saladin's own entourage even admitted that the Muslim troops 'were frightened of them, dumbfounded by their steadfastness', adding that when King Richard took the brazen step of galloping along the frontline – lance held aloft – to see who would challenge him, no one stepped forward. The crusaders held their ground, prevailing in what turned out to be the final military confrontation of the expedition.[9]

The victories at Acre, Arsuf and Jaffa stand as testament to the impact of Richard's martial role in the war for the Holy Land. His incisive grasp of strategy and formidable qualities as a battlefield commander combined to earn the Third Crusade a number of notable military successes, while also helping to ensure that the expedition avoided potential setbacks. It seems clear that the Lionheart relished his role as a warrior-king and delighted in the chaotic thrill of hand-to-hand combat. In part this may have been linked to his fascination with contemporary notions of chivalric virtue. Not only was Richard willing to place himself at the heart of the action during major engagements, such as the relief of Jaffa, he also made repeated attempts to actively seek out opportunities to demonstrate his skill at arms, thereby earning glory and renown.

During a lull in hostilities through the autumn of 1191, he personally led a succession of raiding parties into enemy-held territory. These sorties gathered valuable supplies and intelligence, but they also helped to sate the Lionheart's appetite for action. Not all of them went to plan. During one foray, on 29 September, Richard's company was ambushed at night by a large Muslim force and drawn into a desperate, bloody skirmish. In the ensuing fracas, four Frankish knights were slain. The Lionheart himself was only saved from capture by the presence of mind of another of his companions, William of Préaux, who reportedly called out 'Saracens, I am the king' and allowed himself to be taken prisoner while Richard escaped.* Even Ambroise, who generally portrayed the Angevin king in singularly glowing terms, saw fit to chastise the sovereign for taking such risks, acknowledging that the crusade would be doomed to failure should the Lionheart be lost.[10]

Of course, to some extent it comes as no surprise to learn that Richard the Lionheart made a pivotal military contribution to the Third Crusade. He has, after all, long been

---

* Richard rewarded William of Préaux's loyalty at the end of the crusade, agreeing to release ten high-ranking Muslim captives in return for his release.

remembered as a medieval warrior-king par excellence, with even his most vocal modern detractors conceding that he was brutally effective in the business and practice of war. Less attention has been paid to Richard's skills as a diplomat during his time in the Levant. This is perhaps in part because the surviving Western Christian accounts of the crusade provide little or no evidence of him actively pursuing this role. However, a rich vein of close Muslim testimony preserved in Arabic sources makes it clear that the Lionheart was actually a remarkably adept – and occasionally even devious – negotiator. By the time he arrived in the Near East, Richard understood the value of diplomatic engagement. Every successful European monarch recognized that direct negotiation afforded valuable opportunities to gather raw intelligence, sow disinformation or dissent, and assess enemy intentions. And, regardless of the fact that he would be dealing with supposed 'heathens' – those branded as 'sons of the Devil' by the papacy – the Lionheart had every intention of deploying these more subtle weapons of war during his crusade.[11]

Almost from the moment he arrived in Palestine, Richard looked to open a channel of communication with Saladin's camp. The Lionheart's first priority was to secure a face-to-face meeting with the sultan, probably in large part to gain some measure of his new opponent's character and temperament. Saladin sidestepped these overtures, reportedly arguing that 'kings do not meet unless an agreement has been reached' and adding that 'it is not good for them to fight after meeting and eating together'.[12] In fact, there is no credible evidence to suggest that Richard and

Saladin ever met in person. Instead, the sultan deputized his brother and loyal lieutenant, al-Adil, to speak on his behalf. Through the course of the Third Crusade, the Angevin king met al-Adil on numerous occasions and a degree of friendship seems to have developed between them. In time, their encounters came to be marked by the exchange of rare delicacies, and musicians would play for their entertainment even as the pair angled for advantage.

One of Richard's opening gambits during the summer of 1191 was to issue repeated requests for gifts from the Ayyubid camp, including feed for his hunting birds and a supply of 'fruit and ice', the latter being a great luxury that probably would have been brought by courier from the Lebanese mountains almost a hundred miles away. The Lionheart seems to have been testing precisely how far he could press Saladin's generosity, while also looking to gain a sense of his strength, resources and the morale within his army. A Muslim eyewitness conceded that the sultan entertained these approaches precisely because he too wished to learn more about his opponent.[13]

Richard also used diplomacy to wrong-foot his enemy. During the long and tortuous fighting march south from Acre to Jaffa, the Lionheart became concerned that Saladin was planning to ambush the crusaders as they passed through an area of thick woodland north of Arsuf. On the evening of 4 September, Richard made camp near the fringes of the forest and then despatched messengers to request urgent talks with al-Adil so that terms of truce could be arranged. The sultan let down his guard, imagining that a sustained period of serious negotiation would follow, but once the meeting began it quickly became clear that the Lionheart was in no mood for equitable discussion. Instead, he apparently presented al-Adil with a blunt ultimatum, stating that 'the basic condition (of peace) is that you should restore all the lands to us (that you have conquered) and return to your own territories'. Not surprisingly, al-Adil was far from impressed by this demand for wholesale surrender and promptly broke off the talks. Richard then seized what seems to have been a carefully crafted opportunity, immediately ordering his army to march south through the Forest of Arsuf before Saladin's forces had time to prepare for an attack. The crusaders faced no opposition that day and duly reached their evening camp unscathed.[14]

Both sides used diplomacy to cultivate suspicion and distrust with the enemy camp during the crusade. Saladin made frequent contact with King Richard's political rival in the Holy Land, Conrad of Montferrat – a recent arrival in the Near East, who had seized command of the Christian-held outpost of Tyre and wished to be proclaimed as the new Latin king of Jerusalem in place of Guy of Lusignan.* In October 1191, Saladin even tried to persuade Conrad to launch a direct attack on the crusaders in Acre. That same autumn, while he was laying the foundations for an armed incursion inland from Jaffa towards

---

* Guy's claim to the Jerusalemite crown derived from his marriage to King Baldwin IV of Jerusalem's daughter Sybilla, but she succumbed to illness (along with her two infant daughters) during the siege of Acre, leaving Guy's legitimacy open to question.

Jerusalem, Richard reopened a channel of communication with al-Adil. In spite of their recent argument, the tone of their missives was generally convivial. The Angevin king even described al-Adil as 'my brother and my friend'. Then, around 21 October, Richard made another outlandish proposal: the crusade would be called off if al-Adil married the Lionheart's sister Joanne and Saladin agreed to grant them joint rule over Jerusalem and Palestine.[15]

It is impossible to know whether Richard ever seriously intended to follow through with this suggestion – and, in the end, the whole scheme came to nothing – but he must have understood that the mere prospect of such a settlement insinuated a seed of doubt into the heart of the Ayyubid camp. Had the plan gone ahead, al-Adil would have been gifted power, wealth and territory to rival that of his more famous brother. He certainly would have been marked out as a potential threat to Saladin's eldest son and prospective heir, al-Afdal. Not surprisingly, al-Adil moved with extreme care when relaying Richard's terms to the sultan, aware that any hint of overenthusiasm for the deal might ignite suspicions that he was seeking advancement or harbouring personal ambitions. On this occasion, Saladin was not taken in by the Lionheart's ruse and continued to place his trust in his brother. It is perhaps worth noting, however, that just three years after the sultan's death, al-Adil did indeed usurp power from his nephew, so perhaps Richard had accurately detected the first glimmers of a fracture within the Ayyubid dynasty.

The Lionheart continued to cultivate a close relationship with al-Adil through the remainder of his time in the Holy

Land. The king also made efforts to befriend and influence other leading members of Saladin's inner circle. These included the Kurdish warlord Saif al-Din al-Mashtub, who had commanded the Muslim garrison at Acre, and the Turcoman commander Badr al-Din Dildirim. Both men actively promoted Richard's interests during the prolonged negotiations through the summer of 1192 that finally brought the Third Crusade to a conclusion and acted as guarantors of the subsequent Treaty of Jaffa, finalized on 2 September.

Not all of King Richard's efforts in the realm of diplomacy ended in success or advantage, however. Indeed, his most infamous act during the entire crusade resulted from a breakdown in negotiations. When the port city of Acre surrendered to the crusaders on 12 July 1191, Richard and Philip Augustus took around 3,000 surviving members of its Muslim garrison captive. The deal struck to secure Acre's capitulation specified that these prisoners would only be freed in exchange for a cash payment of 200,000 gold dinars, the return of the sacred relic of the True Cross captured at Hattin and the release of a sizeable number of Christians currently languishing in Muslim captivity, including 1,500 Franks 'of common, unremarkable background' and around 200 named men of rank. Saladin would have just one month to fulfil these punitive terms.[16]

Ten days later, King Philip suddenly announced his intention to depart for Western Europe and the sole responsibility for leading the crusade fell to Richard. From this point onwards, time became an essential component of the Lionheart's calculations. Once his Capetian rival reached France, there was every chance he would try to invade Angevin territory or lure John into a damaging conspiracy. Each passing day spent in the Holy Land only increased the possibility that when Richard did eventually return home he would find his realm in ruins. The Lionheart was also conscious of the changing seasons. In the midst of full summer, it might be possible to press on with the campaign, prosecuting an invasion of Palestine and even a direct assault on Jerusalem. But if the expedition stalled at Acre, the onset of autumn and winter would severely impede any offensive.

With these considerations in mind, Richard had to weigh the need for action against his desire to see the Acre agreement discharged. Needless to say, Saladin must also have been only too conscious of what was at stake, and plagued by imponderable questions. What level of delay might Richard tolerate? Were 3,000 Muslim lives worth more than the chance to stop the crusade in its tracks? Embassies shuttled between the two camps through late July and into August, but at this early stage in the campaign there was still a high degree of uncertainty and suspicion at play. Each protagonist was yet to gain a clear sense of the other's temperament. Negotiations eventually broke down when Saladin began to equivocate over terms of payment, and the original deadline of 12 August passed without any resolution. It may be that the sultan was struggling to gather the money and captives required, but it is equally possible that he simply imagined he could safely string Richard along for a few more weeks. If that was his calculation, then he made a dreadful error of judgement.

On the afternoon of 20 August 1191, the Lionheart marched out on to the plains of Acre, leading some 2,700 prisoners – the bulk of the city's Muslim garrison – all bound in ropes. There, beneath the waning summer sun, he ordered his troops to butcher them to a man in cold blood, and then returned to the port, leaving the ground littered with mutilated corpses. Of all Richard's deeds, this massacre is perhaps the most controversial: a chilling act of slaughter that in the modern era would be classed as a war crime. Some historians have condemned it out of hand as base barbarism – a product of the Lionheart's brutish nature. Others have seen Richard's supposedly intemperate nature at work, arguing that blind rage or impatient fury lay behind the killings. To properly assess the king's actions, however, they must be judged within their medieval context.

A number of significant details emerge from the twelfth- and thirteenth-century accounts of the massacre. Predictably, the view from within Saladin's camp was condemnatory. One Muslim eyewitness described Richard as an 'accursed man', observing that the slaughter was the cause of 'great sorrow and distress'. But the same chronicler went on to seek a rational explanation for the Lionheart's decision, noting that the Angevin king acted only after he saw that 'the sultan hesitated' to fulfil the terms of the surrender agreement, and theorizing that Richard may have been moved to eliminate most of the garrison because he 'did not think it wise to leave that number [of Muslim prisoners] in his rear' when marching on into Palestine.[17]

Perhaps the most surprising feature of much of the

contemporary Western evidence for these events is that it seems utterly unconcerned to defend the Lionheart against possible accusations of senseless or excessive brutality. If the king's behaviour were to be impugned, it was not on grounds of savagery, but because he might be accused of breaking a promise of safe conduct to captives – a dishonourable act that contravened chivalric custom. Richard's own description of the massacre, preserved in a letter dated 1 October 1191, strove to protect his reputation by explaining that when 'the time-limit [for reparations] expired ... the pact which [Saladin] had agreed was entirely made void'. As a result, 'we quite properly had the Saracens that we had in custody ... put to death'. It would appear that what mattered above all to the Lionheart was his reputation.[18]

On balance, it seems unlikely that the Acre massacre was prompted by an uncontrolled fit of anger, not least because the carnage was far from indiscriminate, with all of the high-ranking Muslim captives spared in expectation of their eventual ransom. The killing was, in all likelihood, carefully premeditated – a sudden and terrible eruption of expedient violence, calculated to send Saladin a stark message of intent and to permit the crusade to progress. Even amid the endemic violence of the medieval world, and in the setting of a crusade, such a large-scale execution of captives was unusual. None the less, contemporary reactions to the event should not be exaggerated. In the immediate aftermath of the massacre, Saladin put a small number of Frankish prisoners to death, but the channels of diplomatic contact between the Latin and Muslim camps were reopened within just sixteen days.

Richard brought unrivalled resources, military expertise and an edge of icy resolve to the crusade. How then can his failure to achieve full victory – through Jerusalem's reconquest and the recovery of the True Cross – be explained? To some extent, the crusade's outcome was all but predetermined by the nature of the enemy he faced and the challenge he confronted. In terms of age and constitution, Saladin may have been past his best, but he remained a formidable opponent: resolute in his determination to defend the territorial gains made in the wake of his historic victory at Hattin; shrewd in his appreciation of what it might take to achieve lasting victory in the war for dominion of the Holy Land. The sultan had been unable to forestall the loss of Acre and was soundly outplayed by the Lionheart during the crusaders' fighting march south to Jaffa. But in the face of these reversals, Saladin was wise enough to profoundly reshape Ayyubid strategy.

On 10 September 1191 – just three days after his humiliating defeat at the Battle of Arsuf – Saladin convened a council of war. Surrounded by his closest advisers, the sultan unveiled his new plan. If the Franks could not be stopped by direct attack, then the Muslims would shift on to the defensive, seeking to hamper, and ultimately halt, their advance. The sultan now resolved to play a waiting game, clear in the knowledge that one day soon King Richard and his crusaders would have to return to the West. In line with this policy, Saladin immediately took drastic steps to impede the Franks. On the routes inland, linking Jaffa to Jerusalem, every castle and fortified settlement was dismantled so that they could not be occupied and exploited by the Lionheart's troops. The same radical 'scorched-earth' approach was extended to the town of Ascalon, around thirty miles south of Jaffa. This strategically vital port – the stepping stone to Ayyubid Egypt – was likely to be Richard's next target. Should it fall into his hands, the king would be in a position to threaten both the Nile Delta and the Holy City. Saladin therefore took the painful but necessary decision to raze Ascalon's defences to the ground, with al-Adil deputized to oversee the hurried demolition.

For the best part of the next year, Saladin withdrew the bulk of his army into Jerusalem and largely avoided direct armed confrontation with the Franks. He had rightly calculated that, in a protracted military campaign, the odds favoured the army fighting on home ground. The challenge for Richard, waging a war far from the Angevin realm, on the very fringes of Western Christian influence, was inevitably greater. Assiduous as his preparations had been, there was a limit to the wealth, material resources and manpower that he could deploy in the Levant. If the Lionheart failed to break the Ayyubid army or storm Jerusalem, at some point he would be forced to return home all but empty-handed. This meant that the odds were stacked in Saladin's favour: he could fall back on a defensive strategy, while Richard would be forced to attack.

For all his skill as a general, it is also the case that King Richard struggled to master the art of crusader warfare. The armies who engaged in these Christian holy wars were, in some particular respects, distinct from other military forces. The heartfelt religious devotion that seems to have underpinned the motives of so many crusaders – their dreams of assured salvation and heavenly reward once Jerusalem was recaptured – could fuel ecstatic enthusiasm, empowering these troops with extraordinary resilience and near-feral ferocity. Time and again, crusader forces campaigning in the Levant proved able to endure untold hardship and horror, and showed a willingness to countenance terrible risks in pursuit of victory. The example had been set at the end of the eleventh century, when the First Crusaders survived the tortuous eight-month siege of Antioch and then gambled everything on a headlong march towards the Holy City, and the memory of their deeds still lingered in the minds of Richard's troops.

Crusader armies were capable of staggering – and sometimes dark – deeds, and could overcome otherwise insurmountable odds. But they also were difficult to command and control. Through the course of the Third Crusade, King Richard I began to hone his already impressive skills as a military leader, but he also came to discover, much to his frustration, that many of the normal rules governing the conduct of war did not apply to a crusade.

In mid September 1191, after the successful march from Acre to Jaffa, the Lionheart looked to identify the expedition's next target. With the fighting season drawing to a close, the wisest course of action – in strictly strategic terms – was probably to mount a raiding campaign into Egypt. Inflicting damage on the economic heartland of the Ayyubid realm would rob Saladin of much-needed wealth and material resources, and might even drive the sultan to the negotiating table. But although the precepts of military science indicated this as a preferred course of action, the bulk of Richard's crusading army simply refused to participate in this attack, regarding it as an unnecessary diversion. They had not travelled across the face of the known world to battle on the Nile – their eyes were firmly fixed on the goal of reaching Jerusalem, and from their encampment at Jaffa the Holy City lay little more than thirty miles inland. The Lionheart relented and, through autumn and on into winter, began building towards an advance on Jerusalem. The fortresses destroyed by the Ayyubids were painstakingly rebuilt, defensible lines of supply and support carefully established.

By December 1191, the Latins' incremental incursion into the Judean uplands had brought them as far as the small settlement of Beit Nuba, just twelve miles from Jerusalem. The weather was appalling, with driving rain and freezing temperatures, yet by all accounts troop morale was high. One Latin chronicler noted that the crusaders 'had an indescribable yearning to see the Holy City and complete their pilgrimage', while another eyewitness recalled that 'no-one was angry or sad ... everywhere was joy and happiness and [everyone] said together "God, now we are going on the right way, guided by Your grace" '.[19]

These soldiers believed they were about to realize their cherished goal of launching a direct assault on Jerusalem, but Richard I's inland march was not what it seemed. In fact, the best evidence suggests that the Lionheart never actually intended to attempt a winter siege of the Holy City. His plan seems to have been to mount a combined military and diplomatic offensive, using a build-up of troops in the Judean Hills to apply pressure while angling for a favourable negotiated settlement. Under normal conditions, a stratagem of this type made perfect sense, but in the midst of a crusade it proved to be a disastrous mistake. When it became apparent, in the first days of 1192, that no progress was being made, the Angevin king announced his intention to retreat back to the Mediterranean coast. This decision had a catastrophic impact on Christian morale. Even contemporary chroniclers who traditionally supported Richard admitted that 'not since God created time was there ever seen an army so dejected and so depressed'.[20]

Fatal damage had been done to the expedition's overall prospects for success, but the Lionheart went on to compound this error by agreeing to prosecute another half-hearted advance on Jerusalem in the early summer of 1192, once again reaching Beit Nuba on 10 June. By this point his grip over the crusade was faltering and, wracked by concerns about John's treacherous behaviour in Europe, Richard was desperate to return home. Arguments raged within the Frankish camp, but the king – counselling that the sheer scale of the Holy City's defences rendered any assault futile – eventually got his way. On 4 July 1192, precisely five years after the Battle of Hattin, the soldiers of the Third Crusade began their second retreat from Jerusalem.

King Richard's failure to harness and direct the power of his crusading force contributed to the campaign's final outcome. The strategic wisdom of his decision-making continues to be debated. Some have contended that even if the Holy City could somehow have been captured it could never be held, because the Franks did not control the surrounding network of fortresses and lacked the requisite manpower to resist an Ayyubid counter-attack. On these grounds, it is argued that the Lionheart made the right choice in January 1192 and again in July that same year.[21]

Given the limits of Richard's knowledge, this is probably an appropriate assessment. But with the benefit of hindsight and, more importantly, access to eyewitness reports from inside Saladin's camp, it is apparent that the Lionheart might in fact have been able to lead the Third Crusade to victory. The sultan's strategy of largely avoiding direct military engagement with the Franks had kept his forces out of harm's way, but the resultant inaction placed significant strain on his Muslim coalition. Questions were asked about Saladin's leadership; allies became more reluctant to contribute to the jihad. And, after five years of extended campaigning, even some of the sultan's own exhausted troops were showing signs of disillusionment.

Problems were already apparent in December 1191, when Saladin was able to garrison Jerusalem with only a relatively small force. By the following summer, the Ayyubids were approaching the point of collapse. The crusaders' second advance on the Holy City caused a scouring crisis of confidence, with everyone inside Jerusalem – Saladin included – expecting that a direct assault was imminent. One well-placed Muslim eyewitness reported that, on the evening of 2 July, the sultan assembled his inner circle of advisers and lieutenants. After a long and heated debate, a shocking conclusion was reached: for his own safety, Saladin would abandon the Holy City, leaving behind only a token force. The next day, as preparations began for the withdrawal, the sultan was seen openly weeping as he led Friday prayer in the Aqsa Mosque.[22] Less than twenty-four hours later, the crusaders began their retreat from Beit Nuba. Had Richard but known of the turmoil in the enemy camp and Saladin's plan to quit the field, he might have pressed on to seize Jerusalem. Such a setback could well have shattered the sultan's already faltering hold over the Muslim alliance, plunging Near Eastern Islam into disarray and enabling the crusader kingdom of Jerusalem to be reconstituted. As it was, the Holy City remained in Muslim hands.

In the aftermath of the second withdrawal from Beit Nuba, negotiations to secure an end to hostilities began in earnest. Through the summer both sides continued to jockey for position. Having received an influx of reinforcements from northern Syria, Saladin launched his short-lived campaign to snatch back Jaffa. With that assault thwarted, Richard briefly appeared to be in the ascendant, but in mid August the king once again fell gravely ill with a debilitating fever. Confined to his bed, the Lionheart could do nothing but agree to a peace.

By the terms of the Treaty of Jaffa, finalized on 2 September 1192, the two sides agreed to a three-year truce. Saladin retained possession of Jerusalem, but granted unarmed Christian pilgrims access to the Church of the Holy Sepulchre. For their part, the Franks held on to the narrow strip of coastal territory running north from Jaffa to Tyre that had been conquered during the crusade.* This precious foothold formed the basis of a new Latin kingdom – with Acre as its capital – that would survive for almost a hundred years.

Once he was well enough to travel, Richard I began to plan for his departure. The Third Crusade was far from an abject failure, but ultimately the Lionheart had been denied the outright victory he craved. On 9 October 1192, sixteen months after he first arrived in the Levant, the Angevin king set sail for Europe. As the long journey began, he is said to have looked backed one last time upon the Holy Land, offering up a prayer that he might one day return to complete the work of reconquest.[23] Ironically, his opponent and nemesis died just five months later. Exhausted by years of war and the hard-fought struggle to retain Jerusalem, Saladin passed away on 3 March 1193 at the age of fifty-five. By the time news of the great sultan's demise reached the West, however, King Richard was confined in a German prison.

* For some reason, there seems to have been no explicit discussion regarding the fate of the Jerusalemite True Cross during the negotiations, and the prized relic remained in Ayyubid hands.

with Philip of France.* There was little danger of the Lionheart coming to any physical harm given his royal status
and potential value as a hostage, but there was a real possibility that he might be held for a lengthy period – perhaps
even indefinitely. Captivity was a tried-and-tested method
for removing high-status opponents from the political fray.
Indeed, Richard's predecessor King Henry I of England
had kept his brother and rival, Robert of Normandy, prisoner for nearly thirty years, while the Lionheart's own
mother, Queen Eleanor, endured a lengthy period of confinement by her husband Henry II. Everything now
depended on Richard finding a way to secure his swift
release, because once news of his incarceration spread, his
enemies were quick to act.

In January 1193, his brother John, Count of Mortain,
entered into a treasonous alliance with Philip Augustus,
hoping that the French king might help him seize the English crown. John travelled to Paris and paid homage to the
Capetian monarch for all of the Angevins' continental lands
and, so it was rumoured, even for the kingdom of England

---

* The duke went on to enjoy little success. He was excommuni-
cated by the pope for his actions and later, after being injured in
a riding accident, suffered an agonizing death. Leopold's foot
was apparently crushed when he fell from his horse, with bones
protruding from the skin, and the injury soon became infected.
Once the foot turned black, a decision was made to amputate at
the ankle, but the duke's son was too squeamish to perform the
deed, so Leopold had to hold an axe to his leg himself while his
chamberlain struck it three times with a mallet. He died soon
afterwards.

itself. In the months that followed, the count ceded further rights to a large portion of Normandy, while to the south, in the Loire Valley, he also gave up the mighty fortress of Loches and the city of Tours. John had given his family's arch enemy licence to dismember the Angevin realm. That April, King Philip received the surrender of Gisors Castle, the lynchpin of the Norman Vexin – the highly contested border zone between the duchy of Normandy and the kingdom of France. In return, the Capetian monarch was expected to mount a full-scale invasion of England and put John on the throne. As it was, Philip made little effort to support John's claim through the remainder of that year, focusing instead upon a furious drive to seize Angevin territory. His historic gains reset the balance of power in northern France in the Capetians' favour.

At the same time, John returned to England, loudly proclaiming his brother Richard to be dead, while affirming his own intention to assume the mantle of king. There were some who supported his claim, and the count was able occupy a number of major castles – including those at Windsor, Nottingham and Wallingford – but many remained loyal to the Lionheart. With his mother, Queen Eleanor, championing the resistance, and no aid forthcoming from Philip, John found his path to the crown blocked. By the start of 1194 most of his gains in England had been lost, and John had scuttled back across the Channel.

It was, at this stage, clear to all that not only was Richard I alive and well – he would soon be free. The Lionheart's aptitude as a politician and diplomat did much to bolster his cause. When subjected to a show trial in Speyer in

March 1193, he defended himself with such skill that most of the German court was won round to his cause. Indeed, even a contemporary chronicler who strongly favoured the Capetians admitted that the king spoke 'eloquently and regally' and in 'a lionhearted manner'.[2] Despite his captive status, Richard also worked ably behind the scenes to reconcile Henry VI with a group of rebellious German princes, recognizing that once the emperor enjoyed greater security at home, he would be less inclined to uphold his pact with the French. All of this abetted the dogged efforts by Queen Eleanor and the likes of William Longchamp to negotiate terms of release. A ransom of 150,000 silver marks was finally agreed with Henry VI and, in February 1194, Richard regained his freedom.

The task of reaffirming his authority in England and restoring the now-tattered fortunes of the wider Angevin realm stood before him. Such was the damage wrought by the Lionheart's duplicitous brother, so grievous were the predations of his enduring rival Philip, that this endeavour would consume the best part of Richard's remaining years. Indeed, the struggle would prove, in many ways, to be the defining labour of his life and his finest hour in the field of war.

Much has rightly been made of the Lionheart's estimable qualities as a knight, a battlefield commander and a general. In terms of martial reputation, Richard I stands shoulder to shoulder with England's greatest warrior-kings, from Edward I, the 'Hammer of the Scots', to Henry V, the victor at Agincourt. Scholars now customarily characterize the Lionheart as 'rex bellicosus' – the warlike, or war-loving, king – praising his clinical mastery of the science of medieval warfare.[3] But this trend has also fostered the impression that Richard somehow came to the throne in 1189 with no more to learn about military affairs. Current assessments of Richard's martial achievements generally present his early years as Duke of Aquitaine (from 1172) as the decisive and formative phase in his development as a commander. Having acquired and honed his skills, it is argued, the Lionheart went on to achieve his greatest victories during the Third Crusade.

This approach overstates the importance of some of Richard's successes in the Near East – most notably at the Battle of Arsuf – and underplays the significance of the campaigns he prosecuted upon his return to Europe. In fact, the Lionheart began the Third Crusade as a recently crowned, relatively untested king, and spent much of the expedition sharpening his expertise in fields such as siegecraft, raiding, logistics and overall strategic planning. The crusade may have ended in stalemate, but it was in the fires of this holy war – as Richard I and Saladin fought one another to a standstill – that the Angevin king truly tempered his martial genius. He returned to the West having acquired a new depth of experience and insight, and proved only too capable of putting the lessons learned in the Levant to good use as he strove first to subdue England, and then to reclaim the likes of Normandy from Philip of France. It is this period, between 1194 and 1198, that rightly should be recognized as the pinnacle of Richard I's military career.

Having avoided France by travelling through the Low

Countries, Richard made the crossing to Sandwich, in Kent, on 13 March 1194. Now aged thirty-six, the Lionheart had matured into a remarkably well-rounded leader. He possessed an acute eye for the fine detail of campaigning and the intellect for precise planning, yet retained his appetite for the dirtier work of front-line combat. His ability to inspire loyalty in his troops was unrivalled – he was ever to be seen fighting in their midst, attentive to their needs and at ease in their presence. He also knew the value of reliable lieutenants, such as the knight William Marshal, or the mercenary commander Mercadier: trusted men who could follow orders, but also improvise when necessary. And to top it all, Richard's undoubted charisma was leavened by a hard edge of decisive ruthlessness – arguably a prerequisite for success amid the bloody business of medieval warfare.

All of these qualities were immediately apparent once Richard made landfall back in England. His first priority was to sweep away the few remaining pockets of support for Count John. Chief among these was Nottingham Castle – a stoutly defended stone and timber fortress, well positioned on a ridge overlooking the River Leen. One contemporary even claimed the stronghold was 'so well fortified by nature and artifice' that it seemed 'unconquerable', and up to this point its garrison had stubbornly refused to surrender.[4]

The Lionheart knew full well the tools required to break down Nottingham's formidable defences, and he possessed the organizational infrastructure of logistical support to procure what was needed in short order. While assembling his troops, the king called in his master engineer, Urric, from London, and also summoned two siege engines from Leicester and twenty-two carpenters from Northampton. Administrative records even indicate that Richard ordered a supply of Greek Fire – the deadly naphtha-based concoction popular in the East that, once lit, could not be extinguished by water. He reached Nottingham on 25 March at the head of a large, well-equipped army.

Richard's prosecution of the siege that followed was almost frighteningly efficient. He understood that his every effort at Nottingham cost time and money. With finite crown resources and a long war on the continent before him, the king intended to achieve success in this first encounter with maximum speed and minimum outlay. The Lionheart announced his arrival in dramatic style with a thundering chorus of blaring trumpets and horns, hoping to terrify Nottingham's garrison into immediate surrender. The defenders were apparently 'confounded and alarmed' by the sudden clamour but remained resolute, so the king launched a frontal assault to properly gauge their strength and resilience. There was fierce fighting that first day, with casualties on both sides. As ever, Richard threw himself into the fray – clad only in light mail armour and an iron cap, but protected from missile fire by a ring of shield-bearing guards – and killed an enemy knight with a well-aimed arrow. By nightfall, the castle's main gate had been burned and its outer defences overrun, and a number of prisoners taken.

At dawn the next day, Richard despatched an envoy calling upon the members of the garrison to lay down their arms, but they bluntly refused, claiming that they did not believe the king had in fact returned to England. Richard reacted with a chilling show of force. His siege engines were assembled and dragged into position, primed to unleash a deadly rain of missiles, and a makeshift gibbet was thrown up so that some of the captives seized the previous day could be hanged in full view of the castle. Duly cowed, two members of the garrison came forth to parley that same evening, and by the following morning the fortress had capitulated. The defenders 'threw themselves on the king's mercy' and, while he generally showed clemency, two leading members of Count John's attempted coup were severely punished for their disloyalty – one being flayed alive, the other thrown into a dungeon and starved to death. The Lionheart had crushed the resistance of a supposedly impregnable castle in just a few days.[5]

It is perhaps worth pausing to note that Richard's visit to Nottingham did not presage an encounter with Robin Hood; nor did the king find himself battling against Count John's evil sheriff in 1194. In fact, the idea that the career of the legendary outlaw intersected with that of the Lionheart did not begin to circulate until the sixteenth century. Even though this spurious suggestion had no basis in contemporary evidence, it was followed and further embroidered in numerous works of literature, gaining particular currency through the writing of Sir Walter Scott – the influential early nineteenth-century author of romanticized historical fiction. The best guess of scholars actually working with medieval records is that, if he ever really existed at all, the very earliest that Robin Hood could have been active was at the start of King Henry III's reign, more than twenty years after Richard I's death.* There may have been no meeting with Robin in 1194, but before leaving the region the Lionheart did make his one and only visit to Sherwood Forest, which – according to one well-placed eyewitness – 'pleased him greatly'.[6]

Richard spent the next month reasserting his authority in England and attending to matters of state. A public crown-wearing ceremony, performed at Winchester on 17 April, served as a powerful, visual affirmation of his sovereign might. Clear in the knowledge that he soon would have to dedicate the bulk of his time and energy to a war fought on the continent, the Lionheart took care to select an able representative to manage the kingdom's governance in his absence, naming Hubert Walter, Archbishop of Canterbury, as his new justiciar. At the same time, feverish preparations for the coming campaign were undertaken and the king also initiated an elaborate two-year building programme that would see Portsmouth developed as a major naval base, supply depot and conduit of contact with Normandy.

Funding the continental war placed an enormous burden upon England and seems to have contributed to a significant hike in inflation across the realm. Some contemporaries grated at the crown's exactions and the Lionheart's renewed absence, but in truth – unless he was

---

* A convincing argument has been made that this 'Robin' can be identified as Robert of Wetherby, an infamous brigand who was hunted down and beheaded by Eustache of Lowdham (former Sheriff of Nottingham) in 1225.

willing to simply surrender Normandy and the rest of the Angevin heartlands – Richard had no choice other than to fight. By mid May, the king was ready to set sail across the Channel with a hundred ships, all reportedly 'laden with warriors, horses and arms'.[7] He would never again set foot on English soil.

The Angevin king now faced a monumental challenge. Philip of France had capitalized upon Count John's treachery, snatching what one chronicler described as 'the greatest and best part of Normandy'.[8] Most of the major fortresses in the eastern half of the duchy had fallen into Capetian hands and even the ducal capital of Rouen had been threatened. By May 1194, Philip had almost completed his work of conquest and was locked into the siege of Verneuil – one of the last Angevin border outposts south of Rouen – fast proving that he too had learned a few valuable lessons about the waging of war while in the Holy Land. Meanwhile, the French king's accomplice, Count John, had been tasked with holding the nearby castle of Évreux.

Richard made landfall more than a hundred miles away at Barfleur, on the Cotentin Peninsula, just north of what centuries later would serve as the D-Day landing site of Utah Beach. Jubilant crowds were said to have greeted his arrival, chanting that the Capetians were now sure to be driven from Normandy. In public, the king exuded confidence, but one of his closest retainers later recalled that even the mighty Lionheart harboured nagging doubts through the early days of the campaign and proved unable to sleep. Resolving to take immediate action, Richard led his army on a forced march to relieve Verneuil. Along the way, at Liseux, he was met by John. The count had not come to offer resistance, but rather to make a grovelling appeal for forgiveness. The king was said to have looked down upon the forlorn figure of his brother, trembling at his feet, and declared: 'John have no fear. You are a child and you had bad men looking after you.'[9] In spite of all of John's grave betrayals, Richard treated his younger sibling with magnanimity – resisting any temptation to try him for treason or bundle him into prison. John was stripped of his lands, but permitted to serve in the Lionheart's army and soon turned Évreux over to Richard.

Pressing on to Verneuil, Richard discovered that the stronghold was mere days away from capture. King Philip had used a combination of siege engines and sappers to bring down a section of its walls and was preparing to mount a frontal assault. Faced with this same situation, a less experienced or more headstrong commander might have rushed in to engage the Capetian army directly. The Lionheart adopted a cannier approach. A heavily armed party of knights and crossbowmen were sent ahead to break through the French lines and reinforce Verneuil's garrison. At the same time, a second detachment marched in a wide arc to the east and south, cutting Philip's line of supply. Having been on the brink of a notable victory, the Capetian monarch now suddenly found himself isolated and dangerously exposed to a counter-attack. On 28 May, he initiated a humiliating retreat, leaving Richard free to enter Verneuil and to celebrate an early triumph.

The Lionheart had prevailed in this initial confrontation, but the war was far from over. Assembling every available ounce of manpower, Richard gathered a host of around 20,000 men at Verneuil and began the real work of reclaiming Normandy and the wider Angevin realm. The campaigning in that first year was conducted at a blistering pace. Richard moved with speed and assurance, targeting critical centres of power. Driving south into the Loire Valley, he advanced in force on the wealthy city of Tours. Confronted by the sight of the Angevin army, its populace paid Richard a handsome bribe of 2,000 silver marks to forestall an attack and promptly renounced their short-lived allegiance to the Capetians. The Lionheart then turned his attention to Loches, the site of a famous stone keep, towering more than a hundred feet over the surrounding landscape. After an assault that lasted just three hours, Richard overran this mighty stronghold, taking 220 prisoners.

The Angevin king was like a force of nature when launching a direct attack, but he also possessed a remarkably acute appreciation of the precepts governing military manoeuvres and engagements. During the crusade he had sparred with Saladin's forces on numerous occasions, through fighting marches, exploratory raids and, perhaps most importantly, in the course of the first, incremental advance inland towards Jerusalem conducted in the autumn of 1191. This hard-won familiarity with the subtleties of troop movements and armed incursions served the Lionheart well when Philip Augustus tried to launch a counter-offensive.

In the early summer of 1194, the French king marched his troops to the very edge of Angevin-held territory and took up a position just east of the town of Vendôme, from where he seems to have been planning a full-scale invasion of the Loire Valley. Richard responded quickly – moving his own host into the region and establishing a camp in front of Vendôme. Only a few miles now separated the two well-matched armies. At this stage, Philip must have imagined that he still had the initiative, but he badly misjudged the situation. The Lionheart understood, through his reading of both the surrounding landscape and the relative disposition of their respective forces, that his enemy had overreached himself. If the Capetian king tried to mount a direct advance on Vendôme, Richard could send a portion of his troops to perform a flanking manoeuvre and then crush the French on two fronts. But at the same time, any attempt to withdraw might leave Philip's rearguard prone to attack. Unable to move forward or back, the Capetian king found himself in a trap.

As the reality of the situation began to dawn on him, Philip tried to save face – brazenly warning the Lionheart through a messenger on 3 July that the French were about to launch an attack. Richard is said to have calmly responded that he would happily await their arrival, while promising that if the Capetians failed to appear he would be sure 'to pay them a visit' of his own. King Philip's nerve broke the next day. He ordered a hasty retreat along the road running north-east towards Paris, but his lines soon became disordered. As evening fell, the Lionheart pounced, ravaging the French rearguard and supply train. A large portion of the Capetian force was either killed or taken prisoner, and many of Philip's own prized possessions – including the royal archive and seal – were seized as plunder. Philip himself only narrowly escaped capture by hiding in a small roadside church.[10]

By the end of 1194, King Richard had scored a clutch of notable successes, halting the Capetian advance and salvaging the heartlands of the Angevin realm. None the less, much of Upper Normandy and the Norman Vexin remained in Philip Augustus's hands. The French monarch had been stung, but not conclusively defeated. It would take more than three years of further campaigning to recover the territory conceded by Count John. Not all of this grinding war of attrition went Richard's way – there were setbacks and periods of truce when both sides sought to recover and regroup – but the balance gradually shifted back in the Angevins' favour.

One critical step along the road to victory was born out of the Lionheart's nuanced appreciation of the role and design of medieval castles. The lynchpin of Philip's hold over the highly contested Vexin border region was his possession of Gisors. This imposing stone fortress boasted a doughty outer circuit of battlements and a looming inner keep. Even more importantly, it stood only fifteen miles from Beauvais and some forty miles from Paris. The proximity of Gisors to these major centres of Capetian power meant that the stronghold could be readily reinforced or relieved by a French army in just a matter of days – thus rendering any attempt at a siege exceptionally risky.

Drawing upon his wealth of military experience garnered in Europe and the Holy Land, King Richard conceived an audacious plan to overcome this difficulty. If Gisors could not be captured, the Lionheart would neutralize its significance as an outpost by constructing a new fortification of his own. Of course, this was no simple task. Between 1196 and 1198, the king built a huge military complex at Les Andelys, on the Vexin's western edge, seventeen miles from Gisors. Positioned on a sharp bend in the River Seine so that it was accessible to ships shuttling to and from Richard's recently established naval base at Portsmouth, the site boasted a fortified island to control waterborne traffic and a main stronghold perched some three hundred feet above on an overlooking cliff. This latter edifice, nicknamed 'Château Gaillard' or the 'Castle of Impudence', was a masterpiece of military design. Constructed with the finest limestone, it made use of the most advanced castle technology of the day, including concentric walls and machicolations that allowed defenders to drop the likes of rocks or burning pitch straight down on to attackers' heads. Gaillard was nothing short of a cathedral to war and cost a staggering £12,000 – roughly the equivalent of £2 billion today.

The value of Richard's lavish new complex was two-fold. On the one hand, it protected the approaches to the ducal capital of Rouen. More importantly, it enabled the Lionheart to billet with impunity large numbers of Angevin troops on the very fringe of the Vexin. The king then used these forces to patrol and police the border zone in strength. French soldiers garrisoning Gisors and other nearby fortresses soon discovered that they could hardly step out of their gates in safety. By September 1198, the Lionheart was confident enough of his position to mount a full-scale incursion into the Vexin. He seized a handful of minor strongholds and, when King Philip tried to respond by

deploying his field army, Richard launched his own pre-
emptive attack – pouncing, it was said, like 'a ravening lion,
starved of food' – and promptly routed the French army.
The Capetians were forced to flee to the only point of safety
nearby: Gisors. With the Lionheart chasing at their heels,
Philip and his men made a desperately chaotic and humiliating attempt to pile through the main castle gate. Such was
the crush of troops that the bridge over the stronghold's
moat collapsed and the French king was dunked in the water
below. Richard later proudly boasted in a widely circulated
letter that he had personally unhorsed three prominent
French knights with his lance during the engagement.[11]

Philip Augustus had barely evaded capture once again,
but the tide of the war in northern France had turned
against him. In January 1199, he agreed terms for a new
five-year truce and appears to have confirmed the Lionheart's rights to all the territory he had reconquered since
returning from the crusade and his time in captivity. Richard had been forced to commit the full weight of the
Angevin realm's military might and economic resources to
the effort, mustering all of his own strength, resilience and
martial genius, but the damage done by Count John and
King Philip had finally been repaired.

The Lionheart's willingness to place himself in the front-
line of conflict was arguably the critical factor behind many
of his military successes, but in the end Richard's penchant
for close-quarter combat and siege warfare cost him his
life. In the first months of 1199, the king moved south, using
the lull in hostilities with Philip Augustus as an opportunity to deal with an outbreak of unrest in Aquitaine. In late

March he laid siege to the small and relatively insignificant fortress of Châlus. The stronghold was defended only by a meagre garrison and, after just three days, stood on the brink of collapse. Then, on the evening of 26 March, with the light failing, Richard decided to survey the progress made in the investment. He strode forward, unarmoured save for an iron headpiece, but accompanied by one of his knights bearing a heavy shield. A lone crossbowman, perched on the battlements, spotted the figures and loosed a bolt in their direction. As luck would have it, the quarrel found its mark, striking the Lionheart in his left shoulder. The wound seems to have been mistreated by the attendant surgeon, who struggled to remove the bolt, and the injury soon turned gangrenous. From that point onwards there was no chance of recovery. Having named John as his successor, King Richard died on 6 April 1199, aged just forty-one. His body was buried, alongside that of his father, in the nearby abbey at Fontevraud, while his heart was interred in Rouen Cathedral. After all his many grand feats of arms and far-flung escapades, the Lionheart had been slain by a common soldier in the midst of an all but meaningless siege. This sudden, unexpected end shocked contemporaries. One chronicler recorded that his passing was 'a source of grief to all', while another wrote: 'O death! Do you realise whom you snatched from us? . . . the lord of warriors, the glory of kings.'[12]

Were contemporaries right to mourn the passing of Richard I and to laud his supposed qualities and achievements? When seeking to make a sober estimation of the man and his reign, some of the gravest excesses can be discarded. Richard was no mindless thug. Nor was he a superhuman hero – the titan turning back a thousand enemies single-handedly that we see rendered in so many medieval accounts. But a strong case can be made to suggest that as a king the Lionheart possessed many different faces and an inimitable array of distinct qualities. He was at once a violent and ruthless warrior and a cultured man of learning; a guileful politician, calculating general and diligent logician, yet ever restless for action and neglectful of his own safety. At court he might remain proud and aloof – the distant sovereign – but in the field he was approachable and charismatic, attentive to the needs of his men.

Perhaps these various personas were simply a reflection of the diverse roles Richard was called upon to fulfil. He was never simply the King of England, or even the ruler of the greater Angevin realm. Yes, he wished to be remembered as the majestic monarch, but that was not enough. The Lionheart also aspired to achieve untrammelled success as a military commander, renown as a storied knight and victory as a holy crusader. In part it was the caprice of chance that placed these demands, and opportunities, before him. The early death of his elder brother opened Richard's pathway to the crown. The outbreak of war in the Near East propelled him on to the international stage. And the perpetual rivalry with his increasingly powerful nemesis, Philip of France, forced him to prioritize war above statecraft. But there is also an unmistakable sense that the Lionheart embraced these trials, seeing them as steps along the path to greatness.

In one particular respect, Richard was most avowedly the child and mirror of his parents, for like Henry II and Eleanor of Aquitaine, he was driven by an indomitable, insatiable sense of ambition. But the Lionheart was also a product of the new age of chivalry – not in the sense that he cherished the mannered niceties of courtly life or craved the artificial glory that might be earned on the tournament field; Richard's chivalric endeavours were more worldly. He wished to garner honour through wise rule, force of arms and martial triumph, and lived in the full expectation that these achievements would be celebrated by his contemporaries and memorialized through the ages. In many respects the Lionheart was Western Europe's first true *roi-chevalier* or king-knight. His thirst for power was subsumed by a deeper hunger for fame and renown, and he harboured an acute awareness of his own reputation, actively cultivating his image as something akin to a living legend: both Arthur the all-conquering king and Lancelot the unrivalled champion, made flesh in one man.

Perhaps Richard should not be judged too harshly for his pursuit of recognition, for this same near-obsessive narcissism pervaded much of late twelfth-century chivalric culture and its influence can be detected in the careers of a number of contemporary knights and aristocrats. But there were few, if any, kings or rulers in this day who allowed themselves to be so distracted from the business of govern-ance and dynastic preservation. In comparison to Richard, the men who confronted him as rivals and enemies through the course of his life were a cut apart: in his prime, Henry II was the arch powerbroker and empire builder; Philip

Augustus, the patient and dutiful spider, carefully spinning the web that would entrap his opponents; and Saladin, the holy warrior with a singular devotion to his sacred cause.

For all of Richard's successes and accomplishments, strengths and abilities, in the end he could be accused of having worked, first and foremost, not for the betterment of his realm, protection of his kin or defence of Christendom, but for himself. His eyes seem to have been fixed on the creation of a legend, rather than the foundation of a legacy. Arguably, the quest for this hollow prize placed the Angevin realm on the path to destruction, for in neglecting the issue of succession, Richard I paved the way for his younger brother's rise to power. And it would be King John who brought England to its knees and squandered all the Lionheart's hard-won gains.

5
The Legendary King

Richard I's short but remarkable reign came to an end in 1199, but he was not forgotten. Perhaps more than any other king of England from this era, the Lionheart achieved lasting fame and enduring prominence in popular imagination. His deeds, embroidered and interwoven with myth, have long been celebrated in literature and song, art and sculpture, and now in television and film. And, unlike most English monarchs, his renown extends beyond the British Isles to reach around the globe – whether he is remembered as a warrior without equal, a towering adversary or an icon of national identity. So why has Richard achieved this recognition, and where is the line between reality and invention?

It is no exaggeration to say that the Lionheart has always been the subject of fanciful tales and fantastical legends. Even within his own lifetime, Richard attained a kind of semi-mythical status. He seems to have actively cultivated his own reputation on the international stage, courting celebrity wherever he went. His famous nickname, *Coeur de Lion*, was already in use during his reign, and Richard evidently relished its potent associations with such martial qualities as ferocity and bravery. His father had been known as 'Curtmantle' (short robe), while his brother John would suffer under the withering moniker of 'Softsword'. Richard – as one admiring contemporary proudly pointed out – was 'the noble king, the Lion-Heart'.[1] Many chroniclers and writers, including some who lived alongside Richard, played an active role in promoting the cult of personality that developed around their sovereign – weaving stories of his heroic feats into their accounts, sometimes even imbuing the Lionheart with near-superhuman abilities.

In Ambroise's influential Old French verse account of the Third Crusade, Richard was presented as 'the boldest king in the world', a warrior who could ride into battle 'faster than a crossbow bolt', leaving a trail of vanquished foes in his wake. The poetic form of Ambroise's eyewitness narrative – which drew heavily from the epic *chansons de geste* (songs of deeds) – helped him to mix realism with fantasy. Thus, the Lionheart was shown fighting outside Jaffa in August 1192 like a titan of old:

> The powerful king was in the press, against the Turks and the Persians. Never did one man [make] such efforts. He threw himself against the Turks, splitting them to their teeth. He fought so often; he struck so many blows; he did himself such injury in striking that the skin of his hands cracked.[2]

Traditionally framed chronicles, written in prose Latin, might at first glance be expected to offer a more sober appraisal of events, but the author of the *Itinerarium Peregrinorum et Gesta Regis Ricardi* – another important eyewitness narrative of the Third Crusade – actually drew heavily upon Ambroise's text. He claimed that Richard had been endowed by God 'with virtues which seemed rather to belong to an earlier age. In this present age, when the world is growing old, these virtues hardly appear in anyone, as if everyone were like empty husks.' In comparison, the Lionheart supposedly possessed 'the valour of Hector, the heroism of Achilles' and 'was not inferior to Alexander'.[3]

Of course, sycophantic courtiers and fawning acolytes have a well-known tendency to praise the leaders they serve. But Richard's accomplishments brought him recognition outside his pool of immediate supporters and far beyond the term of his own life. Indeed, even some of the Lionheart's most embittered enemies were moved to acknowledge his qualities. Muslim chroniclers in the Near and Middle East often praised Richard's fearsome tenacity – one who lived through the ravages of the Third Crusade characterized the king as 'a mighty warrior of great courage' driven by 'a burning passion for war'. The renowned Arab historian and scholar Ibn al-Athir, who wrote a grand history of the world in the early thirteenth century, went so far as to describe Richard as 'the most remarkable man of his age'.[4]

Back in Europe, the fascination with the Lionheart only intensified in the aftermath of his death, not least because his character and achievements could be so readily compared to those of his infamous brother and successor, King John. This was also the precise period in which Western culture's obsession with chivalric ideals intensified. Contemporary literature was awash with tales of honourable knights and daring exploits. Many of these stories were situated in the realms of pure myth-history, including that of the Arthurian court.

The Angevin dynasty had shown a marked interest in establishing a connection to – and even the co-opting of – the largely fabricated memory of King Arthur. Indeed, the monks of Glastonbury apparently initiated their search for the great king's tomb at Henry II's behest and went on to 'discover' the remains of both Arthur and his enchanting bride Guinevere in around 1191. By that stage, Richard I had already embarked on the crusade bearing a sword named Excalibur, though he does not seem to have been overly attached to the weapon, as he later gave it to the King of Sicily in return for a fleet of nineteen ships.

For the authors of chivalric literature, and even some of the more inventive historians writing in the thirteenth century, the Lionheart developed into an ideal protagonist – a heroic figure drawn from the near-past who could emulate the likes of Arthur and his knights. Three distinctive features of the late king's career attracted particular attention, spawning an array of imaginative, larger-than-life legends. Some were fascinated by Richard's evocative nickname and sought to explore its origin and meaning. A popular tale examining this theme seems to have been circulating by around 1230 and was later incorporated into the well-known fourteenth-century Middle English romance poem *Richard Coeur de Lion*. This story offered a garbled account of the Lionheart's time in captivity – placing his imprisonment before, rather than after, his crusade and naming his captor as King Modred of Almayn. While in prison, Richard was said to have begun an illicit love affair with Modred's beautiful daughter Margery, but when their tryst was discovered, Modred took his revenge by releasing a lion into the Angevin king's cell. Being the magnificent hero that he was, Richard was unperturbed by this threat – he simply reached down the beast's throat and ripped out its still-beating heart with his bare hands. To top it all, he then bore the blood-dripping organ into Modred's great hall and, pausing only to sprinkle a little salt on the heart, he wolfed it down with gusto before the horrified king and his assembled court.[5]

This legend touched upon the second intriguing aspect of Richard I's life – the fact that he had been held captive in Austria and Germany. Medieval storytellers had long been fascinated by the notion of great men suddenly finding themselves held in confinement, and the Lionheart's own time as a prisoner certainly offered fertile ground.* One refrain on this theme, first emerging in a work composed near Rheims around 1260, gave rise to a particularly enduring myth: the story of Blondel – the king's faithful minstrel. Once Richard was captured, Blondel was supposed to have mounted a determined search for his 'missing' master. This

---

* Tales related to the First Crusade leader Bohemond of Taranto's time as a prisoner of the Turks in Asia Minor circulated widely in the early twelfth century. His eventual release was attributed variously to the intervention of a beautiful Muslim noblewoman or the intercession of Saint Leonard, the patron saint of captives.

saw him criss-crossing Germany and Austria, pausing at the foot of countless castles to sing a song that he and Richard had written together, until finally at Dürnstein he heard the tune repeated and realized the Lionheart lay within. While the Angevin king did indeed compose at least two doleful laments while in captivity, both of which survive to this day, the tale of Blondel is pure fiction.[6]

Above and beyond all else, however, it was Richard I's participation in the Third Crusade and his titanic struggle with Saladin for control of the Holy Land that inspired generations of writers, artists and myth-makers. Played out in the remote Levant, the crusade possessed an intoxicating exoticism. It also matched the Lionheart against the perfect opponent – the great Muslim sultan of the East, the victor at Hattin and conqueror of Jerusalem. In fact, the confrontation between Richard and Saladin catapulted them both into the forefront of the medieval European imagination. Some chose to present the sultan in a romanticized light, emphasizing his cultured demeanour. It was even suggested that he had been dubbed a knight in the course of his career and adhered to the precepts of chivalry. In these tales, Saladin's encounters with Richard were almost always well-mannered exemplars of courtly behaviour. Others painted the Muslim leader with a more demonic face – the scourge of Christendom, crushed by the triumphant Lionheart.

It might be thought that two awkward truths would have intruded into the legends spun around the holy war: the fact that Richard and Saladin never met, or even fought one another directly; and the small matter of the Lionheart's failure to actually achieve outright victory on crusade. But in the course of the thirteenth century these details were readily overwritten, not least because most subsequent crusades to the East enjoyed even less success. Popular tales of a direct military confrontation between the two protagonists, often akin to single combat, seem to have been circulating widely by the middle part of the century. In one version of events that seems to echo the fighting outside Jaffa in 1192, Richard was said to have confronted the sultan in a mountain pass, accompanied by just a handful of knights. In another, the Lionheart faced Saladin in a mighty duel, with both men – mounted on magnificent warhorses – exchanging blows. Here, fiction was providing what reality had failed to furnish: a decisive clash between the two champions; and one from which Richard always emerged triumphant, usually by driving a humiliated Saladin from the field.

The image of the Lionheart defeating Saladin in single combat also found expression in contemporary art. A series of glazed floor tiles dating from the 1250s, discovered in Chertsey Abbey, Surrey, and now on display in London's British Museum, depicts a tableau of this mythical encounter. Here, Richard is the archetypal man of action. Clad in full armour, his shield emblazoned with the royal coat of arms, the Lionheart's body seems coiled with energy – braced for the impact of the lance couched beneath his arm, as his horse leaps forward to attack. Saladin, by contrast, is the enemy vanquished: his unarmoured body arched backwards, pierced through by the sharp point of Richard's weapon; his horse folding beneath him in defeat. The Chertsey Tiles convey a clear impression of absolute victory – one in which the Muslim sultan is no longer merely being forced to retreat, but actually slain.

The power of such images, alongside the blossoming cult of mythology surrounding the Lionheart, bear testament to the intensive memorialization of his achievements, both real and imagined, in this period. The legends of Richard's deeds permeated aristocratic culture and certainly found purchase in royal circles. In 1251, the king's nephew and successor, Henry III of England, commissioned a dramatic wall painting of the Lionheart's duel with Saladin for the so-called 'Antioch Chamber' of Clarendon Palace in Wiltshire (though sadly the site has long been in ruins), and it has been argued that Henry wished to present himself as the 'new Lionheart'. It is certainly the case that, when Henry's remarkable son Edward I came to power, a song of celebration declared: 'Behold. He shines like a new Richard!' Later sovereigns were equally enthralled. In the fourteenth century, Edward III of England and his son Edward, the Black Prince, owned tapestries portraying the duel between Richard and Saladin, while an unusual round helmet, supposedly once worn by the sultan, was listed in the royal inventory.[7]

Perhaps the ultimate example of the Lionheart's power to arouse adulation among later generations came not from England, but France. In the wake of Richard I's death, King Philip Augustus restored the ascendancy of the Capetian dynasty. By exploiting the weak and ineffectual nature of King John's rule, Philip managed to seize control over almost all of the Angevins' continental lands.

The territories that the Lionheart had fought so hard to recover in the closing years of his reign were squandered within just a few years, including the whole of the duchy of Normandy. Even Richard's grand fortress, Chateau Gaillard, fell after a grim, seven-month siege, its garrison starved into submission. Over the course of his forty-three years in power, Philip II transformed the fortunes of his realm, and when he died in 1223, he could rightly claim to have been one of France's greatest monarchs.

By the mid thirteenth century, Philip's grandson, Louis IX, was in power. He too went on to enjoy a long and notable career, later being canonized by the papacy. But in one particular regard, it was not to Louis's grandfather that contemporaries urged him to look for inspiration. Instead, rather shockingly, they pointed to the example set by Philip's arch enemy, Richard the Lionheart. King Louis's companion and biographer, John of Joinville, wrote that while Philip Augustus had been 'much blamed' for his early departure from the Third Crusade, Richard I 'stayed in the Holy Land, and did many great deeds, so that the Saracens feared him mightily'. The Lionheart was held in such dread, Joinville claimed, that when 'Saracen children cried, the women would scold them, saying: "Hush! King Richard is coming!" to quiet them'. Hoping to emulate the Lionheart's stirring deeds, Louis IX launched two crusades to the Near East and ultimately lost his life in north Africa.[8]

By the later Middle Ages, Richard I's status as one of England's most revered sovereigns seemed assured. Some even likened his achievements to those of Alexander the

Great, the Roman emperor Augustus and mighty Charlemagne. In popular imagination, the Lionheart was a totemic figure – an idealized exemplar of English monarchy. His influence remained clear for all to see, with the English royal coats of arms preserving the device Richard adopted towards the end of his reign: three gold lions arrayed against a red background.* But the first signs that the wheel might turn against Richard in scholarly circles were already apparent in the early seventeenth century and, by the time the historian Edward Gibbon was writing a hundred years later – in the full throes of the Enlightenment – it had become common for historians to censure the Lionheart's penchant for violence and brutality, while also decrying his neglect of England. In 1864, the leading medievalist William Stubbs reflected the academic consensus when declaring that Richard had been 'a selfish ruler and a vicious man'.[9]

At this stage, however, the traumatic upheavals of widespread industrialization had driven European culture towards a romanticized re-engagement with its medieval past. In art and literature, the Lionheart came back in vogue – his story told and retold through a mixture of history, myth and pure fantasy. As Victorian England fumbled around in its own half-remembered history, desperately searching for a sense of national identity, some latched on

---

* Richard I was also long credited with bringing the cult of Saint George to England, but it has since been established that the first signs of Saint George's adoption as the realm's patron saint date from the fourteenth century.

to Richard – the peerless warrior and all-conquering crusader – as an icon. The Great Exhibition, mounted in London in 1851, featured a monumental equestrian statue of the Lionheart, sculpted by the Italian baron Carlo Marochetti. Such was its popularity that it was soon decided the piece should be recast in bronze and placed on permanent display – the costs of this work being paid for by public subscription, to which both Queen Victoria and Prince Albert contributed. Since 1860, this larger-than-life image of Richard I has stood in the heart of England's capital, beside the Thames, in Westminster Old Palace Yard. There the Lionheart – sword held aloft, astride a huge rearing warhorse, his heavily muscled frame outlined in skintight mail armour – looks down upon visitors to Parliament and the House of Lords: a medieval king who has found a place in the modern world.

Notes

I. IN SEARCH OF THE LIONHEART

1. Ambroise, *The History of the Holy War: Ambroise's Estoire de la Guerre Sainte*, ed. and trans. M. Ailes and M. Barber, 2 vols (Woodbridge: Boydell & Brewer, 2003), ll. 11314–620; *Itinerarium Peregrinorum et Gesta Regis Ricardi*, in *Chronicles and Memorials of the Reign of Richard I*, ed. W. Stubbs, 2 vols (London: Longman, 1864–5), vol. 1, pp. 413–24.
2. Baha al-Din Ibn Shaddad, *The Rare and Excellent History of Saladin*, trans. D. S. Richards (Aldershot: Ashgate, 2001), pp. 225–6; Ibn al-Athir, *The Chronicle of Ibn al-Athir for the Crusading Period from al-Kamilfi'l-Ta'rikh*, trans. D. S. Richards, vol. 2 (Aldershot: Ashgate, 2007), p. 401.
3. J. A. Brundage, *Richard Lion Heart* (New York: Scribner, 1974), p. 250.
4. Walter Map, *De Nugis Curialium*, ed. and trans. M. R. James, rev. C. N. L. Brooke and R. A. B. Mynors (Oxford: Clarendon Press, 1983), p. 478.
5. *Itinerarium Peregrinorum*, p. 144.
6. *History of William Marshal*, ed. and trans. A. J. Holden, S. Gregory and D. Crouch, 3 vols (London: Anglo-Norman Text Society, 2002–6), ll. 9291–303.
7. Roger of Howden: *Gesta Regis Henrici II et Ricardi I*, ed. W. Stubbs, 2 vols (London: Longman, 1867), vol. 2, pp. 78–83; and *Chronica*, ed. W. Stubbs, 4 vols (London: Longman, 1868–71), vol. 3, pp. 9–12. The details of King Richard I's coronation were preserved in these two accounts authored by Roger of Howden, a parson from Yorkshire who also served both Henry II and Richard as a royal clerk. Howden was a remarkably well-informed contemporary witness to the Lionheart's reign and a participant in the first phase of the Third Crusade.

2. THE ABSENT KING

1. *Itinerarium Peregrinorum*, p. xvii; A. L. Poole, *From Domesday Book to Magna Carta (1087–1216)*, 2nd edn (Oxford: Oxford University Press, 1955), p. 350; Brundage, *Richard Lion Heart*, p. 258.
2. W. C. Sellars and R. J. Yeatman, *1066 and All That* (London: Methuen, 1930), p. 23.
3. 'Historia de expeditione Friderici imperatoris', in *Quellen zur Geschichte der Kreuzzuges Kaiser Friedrichs I*, ed. A. Chroust (Berlin: Monumenta Germaniae Historica, 1928), pp. 6–10; *Itinerarium Peregrinorum*, p. 140.
4. J. S. C. Riley-Smith, *The First Crusaders, 1095–1131* (Cambridge: Cambridge University Press, 1997), pp. 81–105; J. P. Phillips, *The Second Crusade: Extending the Frontiers of Christendom* (New Haven, Conn., and London: Yale University Press, 2007), pp. 99–103.

5. Roger of Howden, *Chronica*, vol. 3, pp. 74–9.
6. M. Routledge, 'Songs', in *The Oxford Illustrated History of the Crusades*, ed. J. S. C. Riley-Smith (Oxford: Oxford University Press, 1995), p. 99.
7. Bertrand of Born, *The Poems of the Troubadour Bertran de Born*, ed. W. D. Paden, T. Sankovitch and P. H. Stäblein (Berkeley and Los Angeles: University of California Press, 1986), pp. 384, 415.
8. Ambroise, l. 5246.
9. Roger of Howden, *Gesta Regis*, vol. 2, p. 90; William of Newburgh, *Historia Rerum Anglicarum*, in *Chronicles of the Reigns of Stephen, Henry II and Richard I*, ed. R. Howlett, 4 vols (London: Longman, 1884–9), vol. 1, pp. 303–7.
10. R. A. Turner and R. Heiser, *The Reign of Richard the Lionheart: Ruler of the Angevin Empire* (London: Routledge, 2000), pp. 100–101.
11. Roger of Howden, *Gesta Regis*, vol. 2, pp. 219–20.
12. Richard of Devizes, *Chronicon*, ed. and trans. J. T. Appleby (London: T. Nelson, 1963), pp. 44–6.
13. Roger of Howden, *Gesta Regis*, vol. 2, p. 7; J. Gillingham, *Richard I* (New Haven, Conn., and London: Yale University Press, 1999), p. 265.
14. Roger of Howden, *Gesta Regis*, vol. 1, p. 292; Gillingham, *Richard I*, p. 263; Ralph of Coggeshall, *Chronicon Anglicanum*, ed. J. Stevenson (London: Longman, 1875), p. 96.

3. THE CRUSADER KING

1. *Epistolae Cantuarienses*, in *Chronicles and Memorials*, ed. W. Stubbs, vol. 2, p. 347.
2. Roger of Howden, *Gesta Regis*, vol. 2, pp. 110–11.
3. Baha al-Din Ibn Shaddad, p. 146.
4. Ambroise, l. 4602; Baha al-Din Ibn Shaddad, p. 157.
5. Ambroise, ll. 6296–622; J. F. Verbruggen, *The Art of Warfare in Western Europe During the Middle Ages* (Woodbridge: Boydell & Brewer, 1997), pp. 232–9; Roger of Howden, *Chronica*, vol. 3, pp. 130–33; Baha al-Din Ibn Shaddad, pp. 174–6.
6. *Itinerarium Peregrinorum*, p. 270.
7. Gillingham, *Richard I*, pp. 173–8.
8. Ambroise, ll. 11192–3.
9. Ibid., ll. 111314–15; Baha al-Din Ibn Shaddad, pp. 225–6.
10. Ambroise, ll. 7068–164.
11. 'Historia de expeditione Friderici Imperatoris', pp. 6–10.
12. Baha al-Din Ibn Shaddad, p. 153.
13. Ibid., pp. 155–6.
14. Ibid., pp. 173–4.
15. Ibid., pp. 187–8; Ibn al-Athir, p. 392.
16. Baha al-Din Ibn Shaddad, p. 161; Ambroise, ll. 5192–213; *Itinerarium Peregrinorum*, p. 233.
17. Baha al-Din Ibn Shaddad, pp. 164–5.
18. Roger of Howden, *Chronica*, vol. 3, p. 131.
19. *Itinerarium Peregrinorum*, p. 304; Ambroise, ll. 7672–5.
20. Ambroise, ll. 7772–4.
21. H. E. Mayer, *The Crusades*, 2nd edn (Oxford: Oxford University Press, 1988), p. 148; Gillingham, *Richard I*, p. 191; T. Asbridge, *The Crusades: The War for the Holy Land* (London: Simon & Schuster, 2010), pp. 490–91.

22. Baha al-Din Ibn Shaddad, pp. 209–12.
23. Ambroise, ll. 12259–63.

4. THE WARRIOR KING

1. Roger of Howden, *Chronica*, vol. 3, p. 195; Richard of Devizes, *Chronicon*, pp. 46–7.
2. William the Breton, *Philippide de Guillaume le Breton*, in *Oeuvres de Rigord et de Guillaume le Breton, historiens de Philippe-Auguste*, ed. H.-F. Delaborde, 2 vols (Paris: Librairie Renouard, 1882–5), vol. 2, p. 112.
3. J. O. Prestwich, 'Richard Coeur de Lion: Rex Bellicosus', in *Riccardo Cuor di Leone nella storia et nella legenda* (Rome: Academia Nazionale dei Lincei, 1981), pp. 3–15; J. Gillingham, 'Richard I and the Science of War', in *War and Government: Essays in Honour of J. O. Prestwich*, ed. J. B. Gillingham and J. C. Holt (Woodbridge: Boydell & Brewer, 1984), pp. 78–91.
4. William of Newburgh, p. 407.
5. *History of William Marshal*, ll. 10268–9.
6. Roger of Howden, *Chronica*, vol. 3, p. 240.
7. Ibid., p. 251.
8. Quoted in D. M. Stenton, *English Justice Between the Norman Conquest and the Great Charter* (London: Allen & Unwin, 1965), pp. 176–8.
9. *History of William Marshal*, ll. 10409–11.
10. Roger of Howden, *Chronica*, vol. 3, pp. 255–6; *History of William Marshal*, ll. 10581–676.
11. *History of William Marshal*, ll. 10993–4; Roger of Howden, *Chronica*, vol. 4, pp. 58–9.
12. *History of William Marshal*, l. 11768; Gillingham, *Richard I*, p. 321.

5. THE LEGENDARY KING

1. Ambroise, l. 2306.
2. Ibid., ll. 11140, 6467, 11502–11.
3. *Itinerarium Peregrinorum*, p. 143.
4. Baha al-Din Ibn Shaddad, p. 146; Ibn al-Athir, p. 387.
5. *Der mittelenglische Versroman über Richard Löwenherz*, ed. K. Brunner (Leipzig: Wilhelm Braumüller, 1913), ll. 880–1100.
6. *Récits d'un ménestrel de Reims au treizième siècle*, ed. N. de Wailly (Paris: Librairie Renouard, 1876), pp. 41–4.
7. S. Lloyd, 'King Henry III, the Crusade and the Mediterranean', in *England and Her Neighbours (1066–1453)*, ed. M. Jones and M. Vale (London: Hambledon, 1989), p. 107; *Political Songs of England*, ed. T. Wright (London: Camden Society, 1839), p. 128.
8. John of Joinville, *Vie de Saint Louis*, ed. J. Monfrin (Paris: Dunod, 1995), p. 276.
9. E. Gibbon, *The History of the Decline and Fall of the Roman Empire*, vol. 6 (London: Strahan and Cadell, 1788), p. 104; *Itinerarium Peregrinorum*, p. xvii.

Further Reading

Richard I's reputation was rejuvenated in the late twentieth century through the inestimable scholarship of Professor John Gillingham, and his *Richard I* (New Haven, Conn., and London: Yale University Press, 1999) remains the most authoritative and readable biography of Richard. J. Flori, *Richard the Lionheart: Knight and King*, translated by J. Birrell (Edinburgh: Edinburgh University Press, 2006), places more emphasis on the role of chivalry in Richard's career, while R. V. Turner and R. Heiser, *The Reign of Richard the Lionheart: Ruler of the Angevin Empire* (London: Routledge, 2000), is particularly concerned with details of governance and administration.

Those wishing to place Richard's reign in the broader context of medieval British history might usefully begin by reading D. Carpenter, *The Struggle for Mastery: Britain 1066–1284* (London: Penguin, 2004), while the Angevin perspective can be approached through J. Gillingham, *The Angevin Empire*, 2nd edn (London: Arnold, 2001), and M. Aurell, *The Plantagenet Empire, 1154–1224*, translated by D. Crouch (Harlow: Longman, 2007).

Richard's preparations for, and absence during, the Third Crusade are examined in J. T. Appleby, *England Without Richard, 1189–99* (London: G. Bell & Sons, 1965), and C. J. Tyerman, *England and the Crusades* (Chicago: University of Chicago Press, 1988). No one has yet been brave enough to publish a modern research monograph on the Third Crusade, but there are substantial chapters on the expedition in a number of recent general histories of the crusades, including C. J. Tyerman, *God's War: A New History of the Crusades* (London: Allen Lane, 2006), and T. Asbridge, *The Crusades: The War for the Holy Land* (London: Simon & Schuster, 2010). The most valuable (if not always the most approachable) study of Richard's opponent Saladin remains M. C. Lyons and D. E. P. Jackson, *Saladin: The Politics of the Holy War* (Cambridge: Cambridge University Press, 1979).

Richard's protracted campaigns on the continent after his return from crusade and release from captivity are chronicled in M. Powicke, *The Loss of Normandy, 1189–1204* (Manchester: Manchester University Press, 1913), while two seminal articles considering Richard's martial reputation are J. O. Prestwich, 'Richard Coeur de Lion: Rex Bellicosus', in *Riccardo Cuor di Leone nella storia et nella legenda* (Rome: Academia Nazionale dei Lincei, 1981), pp. 3–15, and J. Gillingham, 'Richard I and the Science of War', in *War and Government: Essays in Honour of J. O. Prestwich*, edited by J. Gillingham and J. C. Holt (Woodbridge: Boydell & Brewer, 1984), pp. 78–91.

A selection of valuable essays exploring the memorialization of Richard's career are presented in *Richard Coeur de Lion in History and Myth*, edited by J. L. Nelson (London: Centre for Late Antique and Medieval Studies, King's College, 1992), and those wishing to trace further the development of the various legends associated with the Lionheart should consult B. B. Broughton, *The Legends of King Richard I Coeur de Lion: A Study of Sources and Variations to the Year 1600* (The Hague: Mouton & Co., 1966), and M. Jubb, *The Legend of Saladin in Western Literature and Historiography* (Lampeter: Edwin Mellen Press, 2000).

A number of the most significant primary sources for Richard's career are available in English translation. These include Ambroise, *The History of the Holy War: Ambroise's Estoire de la Guerre Sainte*, edited and translated by M. Ailes and M. Barber, 2 vols (Woodbridge: Boydell & Brewer, 2003), *The Chronicle of the Third Crusade: A Translation of the Itinerarium Peregrinorum et Gesta Regis Ricardi*, translated by H. Nicholson (Aldershot: Ashgate, 1997), and *The Chronicle of Richard of Devizes*, edited and translated by J. T. Appleby (London: Thomas Nelson & Son, 1963).

Picture Credits

1. Richard I, detail from *The Kings of England* by Matthew Paris, c.1250–59. British Library, London, Cotton Claudius D VI, fol. 9v (© British Library Board. All Rights Reserved/Hirarchivum Press/ Alamy)

2. Reverse of Richard's second seal from 1198 with mounted figure of the king. Canterbury Cathedral, Kent (Bridgeman Images)

3. Portrait of a sitting man thought to represent Saladin, from a fourteenth-century copy of *Kitab fi ma'arifat al-hiyal al-handisaya* by al-Jazari, eleventh century (Freer Gallery of Art, Acc. No. F1932.19)

4. *The Capture of Acre*, French school, fourteenth century. British Library, London, MS Royal 16 G VI, fol. 352v (© British Library Board. All Rights Reserved/Bridgeman Images)

5. The Acre massacre of 1191, in a miniature from Sébastien Mamerot, *Passages faiz oultre mer par les François*, 1474–5. Bibliothèque de l'Arsenal, Paris (Erich Lessing/akg-images)

6. *Richard the Lionheard at the Battle of Arsuf* by Gustave Doré, illustration from *Bibliothèque des Croisades* by J-F. Michaud, 1877. Private Collection (© Ken Welsh/Bridgeman Images)

7. Entrance to the Church of the Holy Sepulchre, Jerusalem (Nikolay Vinokurov/Alamy)

8. Richard and Saladin in combat, earthenware floor tiles found at Chertsey Abbey, Surrey. British Museum, London (Photo 12/ Alamy)

9. Château Gaillard, Les Andeleys, France (Hervé Lenain/Alamy)

10. Twelfth-century stone effigy of Richard from his tomb at Fontevraud Abbey, Maine-et-Loire, France (Erich Lessing/ akg-images)

11. Equestrian statue of Richard, 1860, by Baron Carlo Marochetti, in Old Palace Yard, Westminster (David Lyons/Alamy)

Index